STATISTICS
OF EDUCATION
Teachers
England and Wales
2000 *Edition*

London: The Stationery Office

Applications for reproduction should be made in writing to The Copyright Unit, Her Majesty's Stationery Office, St Clements House, 2-16 Colegate, Norwich NR3 1BQ.

ISBN 0 11 271102 2

Contents

HIGHER EDUCATION

Introduction

This new edition of "Statistics of Education: Teachers; England and Wales" provides updated information on the teaching force, generally to March 1999.

Tables have been grouped into sections for ease of use.

The team responsible for producing the volume were: Andy Clarke, Dean Franklin, Paul Robinson, Dave Golding, John Pascoe and Richard Campbell.

Explanatory Notes and Definitions

Sources and coverage

1 The statistics in this volume are derived from a number of sources:

Table number(s)	Source
1	HESES 1997/98, 1998/99 and 1999/00, TTA survey of ITT providers 1997/98, 1998/99 and 1999/00
2	DfEE and National Assembly for Wales plans
3-13, 21, 22-26b, 32-40, 48a-51b(ii), 53a-58	Database of Teacher Records (DTR)
14, 16-20, 41-45, 52	DfEE and National Assembly for Wales 618g surveys
15, 27-30	1996/97 Secondary Schools Curriculum & Staffing Survey (SSCSS)
46-50, 55, 58	Pensioner Statistical System (PENSTATS)

2 The Database of Teacher Records (DTR) is the Department's main source of teachers' service and salary records and provides information as at 31 March of the year in question. All DTR data for March 1999 are provisional. The tables compiled from the 618G survey, a return of teachers numbers and vacant posts made by local education authorities (including former grant maintained schools), show the position as at January of each year shown. The SSCSS is a sample survey of maintained secondary schools in England conducted by DfEE in November 1996.

Initial teacher training

3 In order to teach in a maintained school, teachers are normally required to have qualified teacher status (QTS). This is usually obtained by successfully completing a course of initial teacher training (ITT) at an accredited institution whose provision meets the Secretary of State's criteria for ITT. Two popular routes to achieving qualified teacher status in England and Wales are: by successful completion of an undergraduate course of initial teacher training or of a course leading to the postgraduate certificate in education (PGCE). Both types of courses are run by higher education institutions. In 1993 a new system of school centred ITT (SCITT) was launched. This is postgraduate training that is designed and delivered by groups of schools. The graduate teacher programme and registered teacher programme came into force on 1 December 1997, replacing the licensed teacher scheme and overseas trained teacher (OTT) scheme. Table 7a(iv) and 7b(iv) shows those individuals entering teaching through these routes.

Teacher flows

4 In tables showing the movement of teachers into and out of full-time service in maintained, assisted and grant-aided schools and establishments, entry to a sector consists of those who were in service in the sector at the end of the year in question but were not in service in that sector at the beginning of the year. Leavers from a sector consist of those who were in service in the sector at the beginning of the year in question but were not in service at the end of the year in that sector. Nursery, primary and secondary schools are counted as the same sector in these tables.

Teachers in service in LEA schools (including formerly grant maintained schools)

5 The tables cover LEA maintained schools (including formerly grant maintained schools). Under the 1988 Education Reform Act, all LEA schools, with the exception of nursery schools, could apply for grant-maintained status. Prior to September 1999, grant-maintained schools received their funding from the government via the Funding Agency for Schools. The first schools were given self-governing status from Autumn 1989. Legislation introduced in September 1999 meant that grant maintained schools would become part of the LEA maintained sector. The separate types of school shown in some tables are explained below.

a Nursery schools provide education primarily for children below compulsory school age, i.e. under 5.

b Primary schools consist mainly of infant schools for children aged 5 to 7, junior schools for those aged 7 to 11 and junior and infant schools for both age groups. Some areas have first schools that cater for ages from 5 to 8, 9 or 10: these are the first stage of a three-tier (first, middle and secondary) school system. Many primary schools provide nursery classes for children under 5. A nursery class is one so designated by the local education authority.

c Middle schools take children from first schools and generally feed comprehensive upper schools. They cater for older junior and younger senior pupils. They cover varying age ranges e.g. 8 to 12, 9 to 12, 9 to 13, 10 to 13 and 10 to 14. Those for pupils aged 8 to 12 and 9 to 12 are deemed primary, those for ages 10 to 13 and 10 to 14 are deemed secondary and those for ages 9 to 13 may be deemed either primary or secondary. Where middle schools are not separated they are shown as primary or secondary as appropriate.

d There are three main types of secondary schools: modern, grammar and comprehensive. From 1 April 1993, sixth form colleges were reclassified as part of the further education sector and are thus excluded from secondary schools from that date onwards.

6 Teachers who divide their service between primary and secondary schools are shown as 'divided service'. The 'miscellaneous' group includes, for example, those in

camp schools and in centres for English as an additional language.

7 Tables relating to maintained nursery, primary and secondary schools cover teachers who hold qualified teacher status and licensed teachers working towards it and include all or some of the following categories.

a Trained teachers.

b Graduate and graduate equivalent teachers (i.e. those with a university degree or qualification which is recognised for the purposes of payment of the graduate addition to salaries), who are untrained and whose graduation or obtaining of a graduate equivalent qualification either preceded the introduction of a training requirement for graduates or equivalents or who are otherwise exempt from that requirement.

c Teachers with certain specialist qualifications (e.g. in art and music).

d Teachers who were granted qualified teacher status either on the basis of service as uncertificated teachers (or equivalent) prior to 1 April 1945 or under the Schools (Amendment) Regulations 1968.

e Teachers who have undertaken approved teacher training, or obtained approved qualifications outside the United Kingdom.

f Trained teachers who are nationals of a member state of the EC, and are recognised and permitted to teach in that, or another, member state of the EC.

g Teachers who were previously employed as licensed teachers, under the terms of the Education (Teachers) Regulations 1989, and have been informed, on behalf of the Secretary of State, that they are recognised as qualified teachers for teaching in schools in England and Wales.

8 The only categories of unqualified teacher which can be appointed to maintained primary and secondary schools are as follows.

a Students on teaching practice (formerly temporary assistant teachers) – mainly candidates awaiting entry to courses of initial teacher training in establishments of further education.

b Instructors – teachers not employed in a general capacity, but who possess specialist knowledge of a particular art or skill (e.g. music, sport) who are employed only where qualified teachers of that art or skill are not available.

c Teachers on the graduate teacher / licensed teachers scheme and registered teaching programme / overseas trained teachers scheme.

9 Teachers in occasional service, i.e. teachers engaged on a short term basis, are included only in analyses derived from Form 618G.

Special schools

10 Special schools, either day or boarding, provide education for children with special educational needs who cannot be educated satisfactorily in an ordinary school. Maintained special schools are run by local education authorities who pay all the expenses of maintenance.

11 Non-maintained special schools are run by voluntary bodies; they may apply for a grant from the Department for Education and Employment for capital work and for equipment but their current expenditure is met primarily from the fees charged to the local education authorities for pupils sent to the schools.

12 For tables 27-30 the subjects were grouped according to the following classification:

Subject	Includes (for example)
Mathematics	Pure Maths, Applied Maths, Statistics
English	English Literature
Biology	Human Biology, Botany, Zoology
Chemistry	
Physics	
Combined/General Sciences	Integrated Science, Double Award Science, Single Award Science
Other Sciences	Geology, Environmental Science, Rural Science, Agricultural Science, Science in Society
French	
German	
Spanish	
Other Modern Languages	Italian, Russian, Modern Greek, Modern Hebrew, Asian Languages, Welsh
Design and Technology	Design and Realisation, Graphics, Graphic Communication, Craft, Metalwork, Woodwork, Food Technology
Information Technology	Computer Studies
Other Technology	For classes taken by pupils-Combined Technology (i.e. lessons covering both D&T and IT);for teachers' qualifications-other technology subjects (e.g. Engineering)
Home Economics	Food and Nutrition, Dress, Textiles, Child Development
Business Studies	
Classics	Ancient Greek, Latin, Classical Civilisation, Ancient Hebrew
History	
Religious Education	
Geography	
Other Social Studies	Economics, Sociology, Physiology, Area Studies, Archaeology, Law, Philosophy, Politics
Combined Arts/Humanities/Social Studies	Modular Humanities, Integrated Humanities
Music	History of Music
Drama	Media Studies, Communication Studies, Expressive Arts
Art	Art and Design, Creative Arts, Pottery, Jewellery, History of Art
Physical Education	Dance, Outdoor Education
Careers Education	
Personal and Social Education	Health Education, Preparation for Adult Life, Work Experience
General Studies	
General Primary Subjects	
Other	SEN, Vocational Studies

13 The staffing of special schools comprises qualified teachers, student teachers, instructors and certain other unqualified teachers. The latter group are mainly teachers of children with Special Education Needs who were transferred to the education service on 1 April 1971, having previously been employed by local health authorities. They are not included in any of the tables in this volume. Some of them will eventually become qualified teachers after serving for a prescribed period in a special school.

Direct grant schools

14 From October 1980 these schools, with the exception of three nursery schools, (one of which has subsequently closed), were re-classified as independent schools.

Teachers pay

15 From 1 September 1993, the Government introduced a new common 18 point pay spine for classroom teachers. A teacher's position on the new spine is determined by the total number of points awarded. A relevant body, that is, in the case of a school with a delegated budget, the school's governing body, may award points under six headings; qualifications, experience, special educational needs, recruitment and retention, responsibilities and excellence. From 1 September 1996, half spine points were introduced to the classroom teachers pay spine. More detailed information on teachers pay scales can be found in the School Teachers Pay and Conditions Document, published annually by this Department.

16 Head teachers and deputy head teachers have a separate pay system with 51 incremental points. A head or deputy head teachers pay is determined by a number of factors including: responsibilities of the post; social, economic and cultural background of the pupils attending; and the group number to which the school is assigned.

Promotions

17 Table 40 shows the numbers of teachers whose grading on the DTR has been changed either from classroom teacher to deputy head or from deputy head to head teacher.

Vacancies

18 The vacancies information is taken from the Form 618g survey. The number of vacancies are counted on the survey date, which is the third Thursday in January of each year. Local education authorities are asked only to count those vacancies for posts which are full-time, permanent and advertised on the survey date.

Retirements

19 Retirement benefits can be awarded on age ground, if upon reaching age 60, on premature ground, an employer makes a teacher redundant, whether on efficiency or other grounds, or infirmity grounds, where a teacher is aged under 60 and has to retire on ill-health grounds. All retirement data is for the year in which a pension was first paid, not the year of the last day of service, for example if a person retires on 31 March their pension will be paid in April for the first time so they are counted in a different financial year to the year in which they left work.

Further and higher education

20 Where statistics on the further and higher education sector are provided these comprise all full-time teachers in adult education centres, youth welfare centres, and nursery training centres, as well as higher and further education establishments outside the 'old' university sector. Figures for 1993-94 onwards include sixth form colleges. The data for 1999 are provisional. A description of the main establishments covered is as follows.

a Former polytechnics and HE colleges now funded by the HE Funding Councils and FE colleges funded by the FE Funding Council.

b Adult education centres. These are establishments maintained by local education authorities which provide a wide range of courses, many of them of a recreational type, mainly for evening students. These centres were formerly given the title "evening institutes". The majority of the staff of adult education centres are employed part-time. Only full-time teachers are included in DTR statistics.

21 No figures are included for teachers in university departments of education, university art teaching training centres and other university departments.

22 Not all graduate teachers in further and higher education are recorded as such and some therefore appear as non-graduates in the tables. Teachers whose degree entitles them to a salary addition are not affected.

Degree subjects

23 For comparability with earlier volumes, in most tables where subjects are shown, graduate teachers have been analysed under the standardised subject groups of the pre 1987 United Kingdom Subject Classification for Education Statistics. However, where the heading "mathematics" is separately shown it consists of those holding degrees in mathematics only together with those with degrees in mathematics and physics in combination; other combinations of mathematics with science appear under 'other science'. Tables 24a and 24b, however, show the number of graduate teachers in nursery, primary and secondary schools who hold degrees in particular subjects. The subjects of the degree have each been allocated to one of 10 subject headings.

Regional analysis

24 The regions shown in the tables include the local education authorities shown below. Since 1 April 1996, a series of local government reorganisations have taken place in England and Wales. The effects of these changes impact on this edition of the volume.

North East:
Gateshead, Newcastle-upon-Tyne, North Tyneside, South Tyneside, Sunderland, Hartlepool, Middlesbrough, Redcar & Cleveland, Stockton-on-Tees, Darlington, Durham, Northumberland.

North West:
Cumbria, Cheshire, Halton, Warrington, Bolton, Bury, Manchester, Oldham, Rochdale, Salford, Stockport, Tameside, Trafford, Wigan, Lancashire, Blackburn with Darwen, Blackpool, Knowsley, Liverpool, St Helens, Sefton, Wirral.

Yorkshire and The Humber:
City of Kingston-upon-Hull, East Riding of Yorkshire, North East Lincolnshire, North Lincolnshire, North Yorkshire, York, Barnsley, Doncaster, Rotherham, Sheffield, Bradford, Calderdale, Kirklees, Leeds, Wakefield.

East Midlands:
Derbyshire, Derby, Leicestershire, Leicester City, Rutland, Lincolnshire, Northamptonshire, Nottinghamshire, City of Nottingham.

West Midlands:
Herefordshire, Worcestershire, Shropshire, Telford and Wrekin, Staffordshire, Stoke, Warwickshire, Birmingham, Coventry, Dudley, Sandwell, Solihull, Walsall, Wolverhampton.

East of England:
Cambridgeshire, City of Peterborough, Norfolk, Suffolk, Bedfordshire, Luton, Essex, Southend, Thurrock, Hertfordshire.

London:
Barking and Dagenham, Barnet, Bexley, Brent, Bromley, Camden, City of London, Croydon, Ealing, Enfield, Greenwich, Hackney, Hammersmith & Fulham, Haringey, Harrow, Havering, Hillingdon, Hounslow, Islington, Kensington & Chelsea, Kingston-upon-Thames, Lambeth, Lewisham, Merton, Newham, Redbridge, Richmond-upon- Thames, Southwark, Sutton, Tower Hamlets, Waltham Forest, Wandsworth, Westminster.

South East:
Bracknell Forest, Windsor and Maidenhead, West Berkshire, Reading, Slough, Wokingham, Buckinghamshire, Milton Keynes, East Sussex, Brighton and Hove, Hampshire, Portsmouth, Southampton, Isle of Wight, Kent, Medway, Oxfordshire, Surrey, West Sussex.

South West:
Isles of Scilly, Bath & NE Somerset, City of Bristol, North Somerset, South Gloucestershire, Cornwall, Devon, City of Plymouth, Torbay, Dorset, Poole, Bournemouth, Gloucestershire, Somerset, Wiltshire, Swindon.

Wales:
Anglesey, Gwynedd, Conwy, Denbighshire, Flintshire, Wrexham, Powys, Ceredigion, Pembrokeshire, Carmarthenshire, Swansea, Neath & Port Talbot, Bridgend, Vale of Glamorgan, Rhondda CT, Merthyr Tydfil, Caerphilly, Blaenau Gwent, Torfaen, Monmouthshire, Newport, Cardiff.

Symbols used

.   not applicable

.. not available

-   nil or negligible

1

INITIAL TEACHER TRAINING
Recruitment to initial teacher training courses: academic years 1997/98 to 1999/00 by sector and subject specialism[1]

ENGLAND AND WALES

	1997/98	1998/99	1999/00 Actual	1999/00 Target	% diff. +/-	Percentage increase 1998/99 to 1999/00
Primary and secondary						
Undergraduate	10,460	9,630	9,340	-	-	-3
Postgraduate	19,480	18,780	18,880	-	-	1
Of which						
School centred/other non-HEI	670	770	830	-	-	8
Total	29,930	28,410	28,220	31,620	-11	-1
Primary						
Undergraduate	7,800	7,430	7,380	-	-	-1
Postgraduate	5,220	5,640	6,000	-	-	6
Of which						
School centred/other non-HEI	210	370	430	-	-	17
Total	13,020	13,070	13,380	13,150	2	2
Secondary						
Undergraduate	2,650	2,200	1,970	-	-	-11
Postgraduate	14,260	13,140	12,880	-	-	-2
Of which						
School centred/other non-HEI	460	410	400	-	-	-1
Total	16,910	15,340	14,840	18,470	-20	-3
Secondary by subject						
Mathematics [2]	1,540	1,190	1,400	1,810	-23	17
English (inc. Drama)	2,260	2,250	2,170	2,320	-6	-3
Science [2]	2,940	2,410	2,510	2,570	-2	4
Languages (excl Welsh)	1,890	1,740	1,570	2,400	-35	-10
Welsh	50	50	40	-	-	-4
Technology [3]	2,090	1,840	1,830	3,060	-40	-1
History	1,040	980	880	860	3	-10
Geography	900	790	920	1,100	-17	16
Physical education	1,730	1,580	1,290	1,120	15	-19
Art	960	950	850	1,010	-16	-10
Music	550	530	550	610	-10	4
Religious education	680	660	570	640	-12	-14
Others [4]	300	360	270	370	-27	-25
Total	16,910	15,340	14,840	17,870	-17	-3

Source: HESES 1997/98 and 1998/99 and 1999/00 & TTA survey of ITT providers 1997/98 and 1998/99 and 1999/00.

1. Includes Universities and other HE institutions, SCITT and OU. Recruitment numbers shown are rounded to the nearest 10.
   Percentages have been calculated on the actual figure, rather than the rounded.
2. Excludes 300 places under the 'Maths and Science 600' scheme.
3. Technology includes Design and Technology, Information Technology, Business Studies and Home Economics.
4. Others includes Classics, Economics, Social Studies and Other subjects.

INITIAL TEACHER TRAINING

ITT intake targets academic year 2000/2001

ENGLAND AND WALES

	2000/2001[1]
Primary	14,250
Secondary	17,870
Of which:	
Mathematics	1,980
English (inc. Drama)	2,320
Science	2,870
Modern foreign languages	2,310
Technology	2,140
History	970
Geography	1,160
PE	1,280
Art	920
Music	670
RE	710
Other	350
Margin of flexibility [2]	200
Primary and secondary	32,120

Source: DfEE and National Assembly for Wales plans.

1. Revised targets.
2. This is equivalent to the provision the Teacher Training Agency had last year to vire places between secondary subjects within certain parameters, but is now given explicitly.

INITIAL TEACHER TRAINING
Successful completers: calendar years 1990 to 1999 by type of course and class of degree[1,2]

ENGLAND AND WALES   (percentages)

	1990	1991	1992	1993	1994	1995	1996	1997	1998	1999	1999 England only
PGCE											
Class of first degree											
1st honours	3.3	2.9	3.0	3.6	3.7	4.2	4.2	4.8	4.9	5.2	5.3
2nd honours	79.0	80.1	80.6	81.6	83.1	83.3	83.3	85.3	85.4	85.9	85.8
other and unclassified honours	8.0	7.3	7.9	7.4	7.2	7.1	6.0	5.4	4.8	4.0	3.9
ordinary/pass	9.7	9.7	8.5	7.4	6.1	5.5	6.4	4.4	4.9	4.8	4.9
Total	100	100	100	100	100	100	100	100	100	100	100
BEds											
Class of first degree											
1st honours	3.7	4.6	3.9	4.2	3.8	3.9	4.0	4.5	4.8	5.3	5.3
2nd honours	83.4	83.2	83.0	80.9	80.8	84.0	85.9	90.1	88.0	87.9	87.9
other and unclassified honours	4.4	4.5	4.5	3.3	3.5	3.2	2.9	4.1	2.8	3.4	3.4
ordinary/pass	8.5	7.7	8.6	11.6	11.8	8.9	7.2	1.4	4.4	3.4	3.4
Total	100	100	100	100	100	100	100	100	100	100	100

Source: Database of Teacher Records.

1. Excludes those for whom no class of degree is shown in the teachers' record system. These are mainly holders of acceptable graduate equivalent qualifications or non-UK degrees.
2. Excludes Open University and School Centered Initial Teacher Training.

INITIAL TEACHER TRAINING

1999 PGCE Completers: Delay between award of first degree and completion of a one-year PGCE by sex and age[1]

ENGLAND AND WALES[2]

				Number of years delay				
	up to 2	between 2 and 3	between 3 and 4	between 4 and 5	between 5 and 6	between 6 and 7	7 or more	Total
Men								
under 25	990	500	260	50	-	-	10	1,800
25 to 29	180	160	210	270	220	140	170	1,360
30 to 34	110	60	40	30	40	30	340	640
35 to 39	90	50	40	20	20	10	210	420
40 to 44	60	30	20	10	10	10	120	240
45 to 49	30	10	10	10	-	-	60	110
50 to 54	10	-	-	-	-	-	30	40
55 to 59	-	-	-	-	-	-	-	10
60 & over	-	-	-	-	-	-	-	-
Total	1,460	810	560	390	290	190	920	4,620
Women								
under 25	3,410	1,620	650	120	10	10	20	5,830
25 to 29	340	300	500	640	480	280	290	2,830
30 to 34	210	140	60	50	30	40	550	1,070
35 to 39	240	130	70	30	20	10	490	980
40 to 44	150	90	50	20	10	-	300	630
45 to 49	50	40	30	10	10	-	100	230
50 to 54	10	10	10	-	-	-	20	50
55 to 59	-	-	-	-	-	-	-	-
60 & over	-	-	-	-	-	-	-	-
Total	4,410	2,320	1,360	860	550	350	1,770	11,620
Men and Women								
under 25	4,400	2,120	910	160	10	10	20	7,630
25 to 29	520	460	710	910	710	420	460	4,190
30 to 34	320	200	90	80	60	70	890	1,710
35 to 39	330	180	100	50	30	20	700	1,410
40 to 44	210	110	60	30	20	10	420	870
45 to 49	80	50	30	10	10	10	160	340
50 to 54	20	10	10	10	-	-	40	80
55 to 59	-	-	-	-	-	-	-	10
60 & over	-	-	-	-	-	-	-	-
Total	5,870	3,130	1,920	1,250	850	540	2,690	16,240

Source: Database of Teacher Records.

1. 1999 data are provisional.
2. Includes those trained through the Open University.

INITIAL TEACHER TRAINING

1999 PGCE Completers: Delay between award of first degree and completion of a one-year PGCE by sex and age[1]

ENGLAND ONLY[2]

	up to 2	between 2 and 3	between 3 and 4	between 4 and 5	between 5 and 6	between 6 and 7	7 or more	Total
Men								
under 25	900	470	240	50	-	-	10	1,670
25 to 29	170	160	200	260	210	140	160	1,310
30 to 34	100	60	30	30	30	30	330	620
35 to 39	80	50	30	20	20	10	200	410
40 to 44	60	30	10	10	10	10	110	230
45 to 49	30	10	10	10	-	-	60	110
50 to 54	10	-	-	-	-	-	20	30
55 to 59	-	-	-	-	-	-	-	10
60 & over	-	-	-	-	-	-	-	-
Total	1,350	770	530	370	280	190	890	4,380
Women								
under 25	3,160	1,540	630	110	10	10	20	5,470
25 to 29	330	290	480	620	470	270	280	2,750
30 to 34	200	130	60	40	30	40	540	1,030
35 to 39	230	130	70	30	20	10	480	950
40 to 44	140	90	50	20	10	-	300	610
45 to 49	50	40	30	10	10	-	100	230
50 to 54	10	10	10	-	-	-	20	40
55 to 59	-	-	-	-	-	-	-	-
60 & over	-	-	-	-	-	-	-	-
Total	4,120	2,220	1,310	840	540	340	1,720	11,080
Men and Women								
under 25	4,060	2,010	870	160	10	10	20	7,140
25 to 29	500	450	680	880	680	410	450	4,050
30 to 34	300	190	90	80	60	70	870	1,650
35 to 39	310	170	100	50	30	20	670	1,360
40 to 44	200	110	60	30	20	10	410	840
45 to 49	80	50	30	10	10	10	150	340
50 to 54	20	10	10	10	-	-	40	80
55 to 59	-	-	-	-	-	-	-	10
60 & over	-	-	-	-	-	-	-	-
Total	5,470	2,990	1,840	1,210	810	520	2,610	15,450

Source: Database of Teacher Records.

1. 1999 data are provisional.
2. Includes those trained through the Open University.

7a(i)

NEW ENTRANTS TO TEACHING

BEd completers: Calendar year 1998: type of service and sector by sex and age

ENGLAND AND WALES[1]

	Total BEd completers in 1998	Not in service in England and Wales at 31.3.1999[2]	In full or part-time service in England and Wales at 31 March 1999[3]					
			Maintained nursery and primary	Maintained secondary	Maintained special	Independent	Other[4]	Total in service
Men								
Under 25	900	300	350	220	-	20	10	600
25 to 29	400	120	140	130	-	10	-	280
30 to 34	220	80	60	70	-	-	-	140
35 to 39	170	60	50	60	-	-	-	120
40 to 44	120	50	30	40	-	-	-	70
45 to 49	50	20	10	30	-	-	-	40
50 to 54	20	10	-	10	-	-	-	10
55 to 59	-	-	-	-	-	-	-	-
60 & over	-	-	-	-	-	-	-	-
Total	1,880	630	630	560	10	40	20	1,250
Women								
Under 25	5,070	1,220	3,350	380	20	110	10	3,860
25 to 29	1,040	330	580	110	10	20	10	720
30 to 34	450	130	260	50	10	-	-	320
35 to 39	610	150	390	60	10	-	-	460
40 to 44	430	130	250	40	-	-	-	290
45 to 49	130	50	70	10	-	-	-	80
50 to 54	20	10	10	-	-	-	-	10
55 to 59	-	-	-	-	-	-	-	-
60 & over	-	-	-	-	-	-	-	-
Total	7,760	2,010	4,910	630	40	130	20	5,750
Men and Women								
Under 25	5,980	1,520	3,690	600	20	130	10	4,460
25 to 29	1,440	440	720	230	10	30	10	1,000
30 to 34	670	200	320	130	10	10	10	460
35 to 39	790	210	440	120	10	-	10	580
40 to 44	550	180	280	70	10	10	10	370
45 to 49	180	60	80	30	-	-	-	120
50 to 54	40	20	10	10	-	-	-	20
55 to 59	-	-	-	-	-	-	-	-
60 & over	-	-	-	-	-	-	-	-
Total	9,640	2,640	5,540	1,190	50	170	50	7,000

Source: Database of Teacher Records.

1. Includes those trained through the Open University.
2. Some in service teachers may be shown as not in service because their service details are not recorded. These may include; entrants to the 'old' university sector, entrants to the independent sector who are not in the Teachers Pension Scheme(TPS), entrants to part-time service outside the maintained nursery, primary and secondary sector who are not in the TPS.
3. Provisional data. The numbers shown as in service may increase as a result of late receipt of annual service returns.
4. Includes sixth form colleges, further and higher education.

NEW ENTRANTS TO TEACHING

PGCE completers: Calendar year 1998: type of service and sector by sex and age

ENGLAND AND WALES[1]

	Total PGCE completers in 1998	Not in service in England and Wales at 31.3.1999[2]	In full or part-time service in England and Wales at 31 March 1999[3]					
			Maintained nursery and primary	Maintained secondary	Maintained special	Independent	Other[4]	Total in service
Men								
Under 25	1,600	480	130	870	10	100	10	1,110
25 to 29	1,880	590	210	930	20	120	20	1,290
30 to 34	850	270	90	410	-	60	20	580
35 to 39	440	150	50	210	-	20	10	290
40 to 44	290	110	20	130	-	10	10	180
45 to 49	150	70	10	70	-	-	10	90
50 to 54	60	20	-	30	-	-	-	30
55 to 59	10	10	-	10	-	-	-	10
60 & over	-	-	-	-	-	-	-	-
Total	5,280	1,700	500	2,650	40	310	80	3,580
Women								
Under 25	4,630	1,090	1,190	2,160	10	150	30	3,540
25 to 29	3,870	1,040	910	1,750	20	110	30	2,830
30 to 34	1,190	390	280	470	10	30	10	800
35 to 39	1,010	320	290	350	-	30	20	690
40 to 44	750	270	210	230	-	10	20	480
45 to 49	280	120	50	100	-	10	-	160
50 to 54	70	30	10	30	-	-	-	40
55 to 59	10	-	-	-	-	-	-	-
60 & over	-	-	-	-	-	-	-	-
Total	11,800	3,270	2,950	5,100	50	330	110	8,540
Men and Women								
Under 25	6,220	1,570	1,320	3,030	20	250	40	4,660
25 to 29	5,750	1,630	1,120	2,680	40	230	60	4,120
30 to 34	2,040	650	370	880	10	90	30	1,380
35 to 39	1,450	480	340	560	10	50	20	980
40 to 44	1,040	390	240	370	10	20	30	660
45 to 49	430	190	50	170	-	10	10	240
50 to 54	130	60	10	60	-	-	-	80
55 to 59	20	10	-	10	-	-	-	10
60 & over	-	-	-	-	-	-	-	-
Total	17,090	4,970	3,450	7,750	90	640	190	12,120

Source: Database of Teacher Records.

1. Includes those trained through the Open University.
2. Some in service teachers may be shown as not in service because their service details are not recorded. These may include; entrants to the 'old' university sector, entrants to the independent sector who are not in the Teachers Pension Scheme(TPS), entrants to part-time service outside the maintained nursery, primary and secondary sector who are not in the TPS.
3. Provisional data. The numbers shown as in service may increase as a result of late receipt of annual service returns.
4. Includes sixth form colleges, further and higher education.

NEW ENTRANTS TO TEACHING

7a(iii)

BEd and PGCE completers: Calendar year 1998: type of service and sector by sex and age

ENGLAND AND WALES [1]

	Total BEd and PGCE completers in 1998	Not in service in England and Wales at 31.3.1999[2]	In full or part-time service in England and Wales at 31 March 1999[3]					
			Maintained nursery and primary	Maintained secondary	Maintained special	Independent	Other[4]	Total in service
Men								
Under 25	2,500	790	470	1,090	10	120	20	1,710
25 to 29	2,280	710	340	1,050	20	130	30	1,570
30 to 34	1,070	350	150	480	10	60	20	720
35 to 39	620	210	100	270	10	20	10	410
40 to 44	410	160	50	170	-	10	10	250
45 to 49	200	80	10	100	-	-	10	120
50 to 54	80	30	-	40	-	-	-	40
55 to 59	10	10	-	10	-	-	-	10
60 & over	-	-	-	-	-	-	-	-
Total	7,160	2,330	1,130	3,210	50	350	100	4,840
Women								
Under 25	9,700	2,310	4,540	2,540	30	250	40	7,400
25 to 29	4,910	1,370	1,490	1,860	30	130	40	3,550
30 to 34	1,640	510	540	520	10	30	20	1,120
35 to 39	1,620	470	690	410	10	30	20	1,150
40 to 44	1,180	410	460	270	10	10	20	770
45 to 49	410	170	120	110	-	10	-	240
50 to 54	100	40	20	30	-	-	-	60
55 to 59	10	-	-	-	-	-	-	-
60 & over	-	-	-	-	-	-	-	-
Total	19,560	5,280	7,860	5,730	90	460	140	14,280
Men and Women								
Under 25	12,200	3,090	5,010	3,630	40	380	60	9,110
25 to 29	7,190	2,070	1,840	2,910	50	250	70	5,120
30 to 34	2,700	860	690	1,010	20	100	40	1,850
35 to 39	2,240	690	780	680	20	50	30	1,560
40 to 44	1,590	560	510	440	10	30	30	1,020
45 to 49	610	250	130	200	-	10	10	360
50 to 54	170	70	20	70	-	10	-	100
55 to 59	20	10	-	10	-	-	-	10
60 & over	-	-	-	-	-	-	-	-
Total	26,730	7,610	8,990	8,940	140	820	240	19,120

Source: Database of Teacher Records.

1. Includes those trained through the Open University.
2. Some in service teachers may be shown as not in service because their service details are not recorded. These may include;
   entrants to the 'old' university sector, entrants to the independent sector who are not in the Teachers Pension Scheme(TPS),
   entrants to part-time service outside the maintained nursery, primary and secondary sector who are not in the TPS.
3. Provisional data. The numbers shown as in service may increase as a result of late receipt of annual service returns.
4. Includes sixth form colleges, further and higher education.

NEW ENTRANTS TO TEACHING

7a(iv)

Employment based route completers: Calendar year 1998: type of service and sector by sex and age

ENGLAND AND WALES[1]

	Total employment based route completers in 1998	Not in service in England and Wales at 31.3.1999[2]	In full or part-time service in England and Wales at 31 March 1999[3]					
			Maintained nursery and primary	Maintained secondary	Maintained special	Independent	Other[4]	Total in service
Men								
Under 25	-	-	-	-	-	-	-	-
25 to 29	20	-	-	10	-	-	-	20
30 to 34	20	10	10	10	-	-	-	10
35 to 39	20	10	-	10	-	-	-	10
40 to 44	10	-	-	-	-	-	-	-
45 to 49	10	-	-	10	-	-	-	10
50 to 54	10	-	-	10	-	-	-	10
55 to 59	-	-	-	-	-	-	-	-
60 & over	-	-	-	-	-	-	-	-
Total	80	20	10	40	-	-	-	60
Women								
Under 25	-	-	-	-	-	-	-	-
25 to 29	50	10	20	20	10	-	-	40
30 to 34	50	10	10	20	-	-	-	30
35 to 39	30	-	10	10	-	-	-	30
40 to 44	50	-	20	30	-	-	-	50
45 to 49	30	10	-	10	-	-	-	20
50 to 54	10	-	-	10	-	-	-	10
55 to 59	-	-	-	-	-	-	-	-
60 & over	-	-	-	-	-	-	-	-
Total	230	40	70	100	20	-	-	190
Men and Women								
Under 25	-	-	-	-	-	-	-	-
25 to 29	80	10	20	30	10	-	-	60
30 to 34	70	20	20	30	-	-	-	50
35 to 39	50	10	20	20	-	-	-	40
40 to 44	60	10	20	30	-	-	-	50
45 to 49	40	10	-	20	-	-	-	30
50 to 54	20	-	-	10	-	-	-	20
55 to 59	10	-	-	-	-	-	-	-
60 & over	-	-	-	-	-	-	-	-
Total	310	60	80	150	20	-	-	250

Source: Database of Teacher Records.

1. Includes those trained through the Open University.
2. Some in service teachers may be shown as not in service because their service details are not recorded. These may include;
   entrants to the 'old' university sector, entrants to the independent sector who are not in the Teachers Pension Scheme(TPS),
   entrants to part-time service outside the maintained nursery, primary and secondary sector who are not in the TPS.
3. Provisional data. The numbers shown as in service may increase as a result of late receipt of annual service returns.
4. Includes sixth form colleges, further and higher education.

NEW ENTRANTS TO TEACHING

BEd completers: Calendar year 1998: type of service and sector by sex and age

ENGLAND AND WALES[1]

	Total BEd completers in 1998	Not in service in England at 31.3.1999[2]	In full or part-time service in England at 31 March 1999[3]					
			Maintained nursery and primary	Maintained secondary	Maintained special	Independent	Other[4]	Total in service
Men								
Under 25	820	280	300	210	-	20	10	540
25 to 29	360	110	120	120	-	10	-	250
30 to 34	200	70	50	70	-	-	-	130
35 to 39	160	50	40	60	-	-	-	110
40 to 44	110	40	30	40	-	-	-	70
45 to 49	50	10	10	30	-	-	-	30
50 to 54	20	10	-	10	-	-	-	10
55 to 59	-	-	-	-	-	-	-	-
60 & over	-	-	-	-	-	-	-	-
Total	1,720	580	550	530	10	40	20	1,140
Women								
Under 25	4,640	1,070	3,090	350	10	100	10	3,570
25 to 29	970	290	560	100	-	10	10	680
30 to 34	420	110	250	50	-	-	-	310
35 to 39	590	140	380	50	10	-	-	450
40 to 44	410	120	240	30	-	-	-	290
45 to 49	120	50	70	10	-	-	-	80
50 to 54	20	10	10	-	-	-	-	10
55 to 59	-	-	-	-	-	-	-	-
60 & over	-	-	-	-	-	-	-	-
Total	7,170	1,790	4,610	590	40	130	20	5,370
Men and Women								
Under 25	5,460	1,360	3,390	560	20	120	10	4,100
25 to 29	1,330	400	680	210	10	20	10	930
30 to 34	620	180	300	120	10	10	10	440
35 to 39	750	190	430	110	10	-	10	560
40 to 44	520	160	270	70	10	10	10	350
45 to 49	170	60	80	30	-	-	-	110
50 to 54	40	20	10	10	-	-	-	20
55 to 59	-	-	-	-	-	-	-	-
60 & over	-	-	-	-	-	-	-	-
Total	8,890	2,370	5,160	1,110	50	160	40	6,520

Source: Database of Teacher Records.

1. Includes those trained through the Open University.
2. Some in service teachers may be shown as not in service because their service details are not recorded. These may include; entrants to the 'old' university sector, entrants to the independent sector who are not in the Teachers Pension Scheme(TPS), entrants to part-time service outside the maintained nursery, primary and secondary sector who are not in the TPS.
3. Provisional data. The numbers shown as in service may increase as a result of late receipt of annual service returns.
4. Includes sixth form colleges, further and higher education.

NEW ENTRANTS TO TEACHING

7b(ii)

PGCE completers: Calendar year 1998: type of service and sector by sex and age

ENGLAND ONLY[1]

	Total PGCE completers in 1998	Not in service in England at 31.3.1999[2]	In full or part-time service in England at 31 March 1999[3]					
			Maintained nursery and primary	Maintained secondary	Maintained special	Independent	Other[4]	Total in service
Men								
Under 25	1,420	420	100	780	10	100	10	990
25 to 29	1,710	540	180	850	20	110	20	1,180
30 to 34	800	250	90	380	-	60	20	540
35 to 39	430	150	50	200	-	20	10	280
40 to 44	280	110	20	130	-	10	10	170
45 to 49	140	60	-	60	-	-	10	80
50 to 54	60	20	-	30	-	-	-	30
55 to 59	10	10	-	10	-	-	-	10
60 & over	-	-	-	-	-	-	-	-
Total	4,840	1,560	440	2,430	40	300	70	3,280
Women								
Under 25	4,120	940	1,040	1,970	10	140	20	3,180
25 to 29	3,600	950	840	1,650	20	100	30	2,650
30 to 34	1,120	360	260	450	10	30	10	760
35 to 39	970	310	280	330	-	20	20	660
40 to 44	730	260	210	220	-	10	20	470
45 to 49	270	120	50	90	-	-	-	150
50 to 54	70	30	10	30	-	-	-	40
55 to 59	10	-	-	-	-	-	-	-
60 & over	-	-	-	-	-	-	-	-
Total	10,890	2,990	2,700	4,740	40	310	100	7,900
Men and Women								
Under 25	5,540	1,370	1,150	2,740	20	230	30	4,170
25 to 29	5,320	1,490	1,020	2,500	40	220	50	3,830
30 to 34	1,920	620	350	830	10	90	30	1,300
35 to 39	1,390	460	330	530	10	50	20	940
40 to 44	1,010	370	240	350	10	20	30	640
45 to 49	410	180	50	160	-	10	10	230
50 to 54	130	50	10	60	-	-	-	80
55 to 59	20	10	-	10	-	-	-	10
60 & over	-	-	-	-	-	-	-	-
Total	15,730	4,540	3,150	7,170	80	620	170	11,190

Source: Database of Teacher Records.

1. Includes those trained through the Open University.
2. Some in service teachers may be shown as not in service because their service details are not recorded. These may include; entrants to the 'old' university sector, entrants to the independent sector who are not in the Teachers Pension Scheme(TPS), entrants to part-time service outside the maintained nursery, primary and secondary sector who are not in the TPS.
3. Provisional data. The numbers shown as in service may increase as a result of late receipt of annual service returns.
4. Includes sixth form colleges, further and higher education.

NEW ENTRANTS TO TEACHING

BEd and PGCE completers: Calendar year 1998: type of service and sector by sex and age

ENGLAND ONLY[1]

	Total BEd and PGCE completers in 1998	Not in service in England at 31.3.1999[2]	In full or part-time service in England at 31 March 1999[3]					
			Maintained nursery and primary	Maintained secondary	Maintained special	Independent	Other[4]	Total in service
Men								
Under 25	2,260	710	400	1,010	10	120	20	1,550
25 to 29	2,100	650	300	980	20	120	20	1,450
30 to 34	1,000	320	140	460	10	60	20	680
35 to 39	590	200	90	260	10	20	10	390
40 to 44	390	150	50	170	-	10	10	240
45 to 49	190	80	10	90	-	-	10	110
50 to 54	70	30	-	40	-	-	-	40
55 to 59	10	10	-	10	-	-	-	10
60 & over	-	-	-	-	-	-	-	-
Total	6,610	2,130	990	3,000	50	340	90	4,470
Women								
Under 25	8,790	2,010	4,140	2,340	20	240	30	6,780
25 to 29	4,600	1,250	1,400	1,770	30	120	40	3,350
30 to 34	1,550	480	520	500	10	30	20	1,070
35 to 39	1,560	450	670	390	10	30	20	1,110
40 to 44	1,140	390	450	260	10	10	20	760
45 to 49	400	170	120	100	-	10	-	230
50 to 54	100	40	20	30	-	-	-	60
55 to 59	10	-	-	-	-	-	-	-
60 & over	-	-	-	-	-	-	-	-
Total	18,130	4,780	7,320	5,390	80	440	120	13,350
Men and Women								
Under 25	11,050	2,720	4,540	3,350	30	360	50	8,330
25 to 29	6,690	1,890	1,700	2,750	50	240	60	4,800
30 to 34	2,550	800	650	960	10	100	40	1,750
35 to 39	2,150	650	760	650	10	50	30	1,500
40 to 44	1,530	530	500	430	10	30	30	1,000
45 to 49	590	240	130	190	-	10	10	340
50 to 54	170	70	20	60	-	10	-	100
55 to 59	20	10	-	10	-	-	-	10
60 & over	-	-	-	-	-	-	-	-
Total	24,740	6,920	8,310	8,390	130	780	210	17,820

Source: Database of Teacher Records.

1. Includes those trained through the Open University.
2. Some in service teachers may be shown as not in service because their service details are not recorded. These may include; entrants to the 'old' university sector, entrants to the independent sector who are not in the Teachers Pension Scheme(TPS), entrants to part-time service outside the maintained nursery, primary and secondary sector who are not in the TPS.
3. Provisional data. The numbers shown as in service may increase as a result of late receipt of annual service returns.
4. Includes sixth form colleges, further and higher education.

NEW ENTRANTS TO TEACHING

7b(iv)

Employment based route completers: Calendar year 1998: type of service and sector by sex and age

ENGLAND ONLY[1]

	Total employment based route completers in 1998	Not in service in England at 31.3.1999[2]	In full or part-time service in England at 31 March 1999[3]					
			Maintained nursery and primary	Maintained secondary	Maintained special	Independent	Other[4]	Total in service
Men								
Under 25	-	-	-	-	-	-	-	-
25 to 29	20	-	-	10	-	-	-	20
30 to 34	20	10	10	10	-	-	-	10
35 to 39	20	10	-	10	-	-	-	10
40 to 44	10	-	-	-	-	-	-	-
45 to 49	10	-	-	10	-	-	-	10
50 to 54	10	-	-	10	-	-	-	10
55 to 59	-	-	-	-	-	-	-	-
60 & over	-	-	-	-	-	-	-	-
Total	80	20	10	40	-	-	-	60
Women								
Under 25	-	-	-	-	-	-	-	-
25 to 29	50	10	20	20	10	-	-	40
30 to 34	50	10	10	20	-	-	-	30
35 to 39	30	-	10	10	-	-	-	30
40 to 44	50	-	20	30	-	-	-	50
45 to 49	30	10	-	10	-	-	-	20
50 to 54	10	-	-	10	-	-	-	10
55 to 59	-	-	-	-	-	-	-	-
60 & over	-	-	-	-	-	-	-	-
Total	230	40	70	100	20	-	-	190
Men and Women								
Under 25	-	-	-	-	-	-	-	-
25 to 29	80	10	20	30	10	-	-	60
30 to 34	70	20	20	30	-	-	-	50
35 to 39	50	10	20	20	-	-	-	40
40 to 44	60	10	20	30	-	-	-	50
45 to 49	40	10	-	20	-	-	-	30
50 to 54	20	-	-	10	-	-	-	20
55 to 59	-	-	-	-	-	-	-	-
60 & over	-	-	-	-	-	-	-	-
Total	310	60	80	150	20	-	-	250

Source: Database of Teacher Records.

1. Includes those trained through the Open University.
2. Some in service teachers may be shown as not in service because their service details are not recorded. These may include; entrants to the 'old' university sector, entrants to the independent sector who are not in the Teachers Pension Scheme(TPS), entrants to part-time service outside the maintained nursery, primary and secondary sector who are not in the TPS.
3. Provisional data. The numbers shown as in service may increase as a result of late receipt of annual service returns.
4. Includes sixth form colleges, further and higher education.

NEW ENTRANTS TO TEACHING

ITT completers in calendar year 1998 in full or part-time service in the maintained nursery, primary and secondary sector at 31 March 1999: region and sector of service by region of ITT

ENGLAND AND WALES[1]

| | Region of service at 31 March 1999[2] | | | | | | | | | | | |
	North East	North West	Yorkshire and The Humber	East Midlands	West Midlands	East of England	London	South East	South West	England	Wales	England and Wales
Government Office Region of ITT												
Nursery & Primary												
North East	310	10	20	10	10	10	20	10	-	410	-	410
North West	40	820	70	50	90	40	90	50	20	1,250	10	1,260
Yorkshire and The Humber	50	110	500	90	30	40	60	30	10	920	-	920
East Midlands	10	30	60	430	60	90	50	50	10	780	-	780
West Midlands	-	20	10	40	550	40	40	40	20	760	-	760
East of England	-	10	10	30	20	460	110	70	10	710	-	710
London	-	-	-	20	10	100	900	260	30	1,320	-	1,320
South East	-	10	10	20	30	70	120	780	100	1,130	10	1,140
South West	-	10	10	20	50	50	100	130	490	850	-	860
England	420	1,020	680	690	840	890	1,490	1,410	670	8,120	30	8,150
Wales	-	40	10	10	40	40	50	60	30	290	380	670
Open University	10	20	10	10	20	40	20	30	10	160	-	160
England and Wales[1]	430	1,080	710	720	900	970	1,560	1,500	710	8,570	410	8,990
Secondary												
North East	330	20	20	10	10	30	10	20	10	460	-	460
North West	30	800	40	50	90	50	70	60	20	1,210	20	1,230
Yorkshire and The Humber	40	110	580	120	50	60	50	50	10	1,070	-	1,070
East Midlands	10	20	20	310	80	60	20	50	10	570	10	580
West Midlands	10	30	10	40	560	50	30	50	30	800	20	820
East of England	10	10	10	40	20	420	70	80	20	680	-	680
London	-	20	-	20	10	160	840	250	20	1,320	-	1,320
South East	-	10	10	30	30	80	110	660	70	990	-	990
South West	-	10	20	20	70	70	50	160	510	910	50	960
England	430	1,020	710	640	930	970	1,250	1,380	690	8,010	100	8,110
Wales	-	20	-	10	30	30	20	40	30	180	380	550
Open University	10	20	20	10	60	40	20	50	30	260	10	270
England and Wales[1]	440	1,060	730	660	1,010	1,040	1,300	1,460	740	8,450	490	8,940

Source: Database of Teacher Records.

1. Includes those trained through the Open University.
2. Provisional data. The numbers shown as in service may increase as a result of late receipt of annual service returns.

NEW ENTRANTS TO TEACHING

Salary ranges and average salary of new entrants[1] to full-time teaching by sector, sex and age, March 1999[2]

ENGLAND AND WALES

	Not Known	£11,000 -£12,999	£13,000 -£14,999	£15,000 -£18,999	£19,000 and over	Total	Average salary (£)
Nursery and primary							
Men							
Under 25	10	-	40	440	-	500	15,260
25-29	10	-	20	400	10	440	15,700
30-34	10	-	10	160	10	190	16,190
35-39	10	-	10	100	10	130	16,770
40-49	-	-	-	70	10	80	16,550
50 and over	-	-	-	-	-	10	18,160
All ages	40	10	80	1,170	40	1,340	15,760
Women							
Under 25	140	10	150	4,540	-	4,840	15,360
25-29	50	-	90	1,810	50	2,010	15,850
30-34	20	10	20	580	40	670	16,250
35-39	30	-	30	640	40	740	16,150
40-49	30	10	40	560	70	710	16,350
50 and over	-	-	-	30	10	40	17,270
All ages	280	30	350	8,150	200	9,000	15,690
Men and Women	320	30	430	9,330	250	10,350	15,700
Secondary							
Men							
Under 25	60	-	90	990	-	1,150	15,230
25-29	40	10	100	1,100	40	1,290	15,780
30-34	20	-	30	470	50	570	16,530
35-39	10	-	10	230	50	310	17,050
40-49	20	-	10	210	70	300	17,760
50 and over	-	-	-	30	10	50	18,210
All ages	160	10	230	3,040	230	3,670	16,030
Women							
Under 25	110	-	120	2,370	-	2,600	15,310
25-29	100	10	130	1,830	50	2,110	15,830
30-34	30	-	20	480	60	580	16,610
35-39	30	-	20	290	40	380	16,670
40-49	30	-	10	260	60	370	17,230
50 and over	-	-	-	20	-	40	18,250
All ages	310	10	290	5,250	220	6,070	15,830
Men and Women	460	20	530	8,280	450	9,740	15,900
Nursery, primary and secondary schools							
Men	200	20	320	4,210	270	5,010	15,950
Women	580	40	640	13,400	420	15,080	15,740
Men and Women	780	50	950	17,610	690	20,080	15,790

Source: Database of Teacher Records.

1. Some teachers classed as new entrants by the DTR may have experience outside the scope of the Teachers Pension Scheme.
   This may explain the higher average salaries for older teachers.
2. Provisional data. Includes some teachers projected as entering full-time service, but whose salary is not known and hence
   excluded from the average salary calculation.

9b NEW ENTRANTS TO TEACHING

Salary ranges and average salary of new entrants[1] to full-time teaching by sector, sex and age, March 1999[2]

ENGLAND ONLY

	Not Known	£11,000 -£12,999	£13,000 -£14,999	£15,000 -£18,999	£19,000 and over	Total	Average salary (£)
Nursery and primary							
Men							
Under 25	10	-	40	400	-	450	15,280
25-29	10	-	20	370	10	410	15,730
30-34	-	-	10	150	10	170	16,220
35-39	10	-	10	100	10	120	16,850
40-49	-	-	-	70	10	80	16,540
50 and over	-	-	-	-	-	10	18,160
All ages	30	10	70	1,090	40	1,240	15,800
Women							
Under 25	130	10	150	4,290	-	4,570	15,380
25-29	50	-	90	1,710	50	1,890	15,870
30-34	20	10	20	570	40	650	16,260
35-39	30	-	30	610	30	710	16,160
40-49	30	10	40	550	70	690	16,310
50 and over	-	-	-	30	10	40	17,270
All ages	250	30	330	7,750	200	8,550	15,700
Men and Women	270	30	400	8,850	240	9,790	15,720
Secondary							
Men							
Under 25	60	-	80	940	-	1,080	15,250
25-29	30	10	90	1,050	40	1,220	15,810
30-34	20	-	30	440	50	540	16,590
35-39	10	-	10	220	50	300	17,110
40-49	10	-	10	200	70	290	17,810
50 and over	-	-	-	30	10	50	18,190
All ages	140	10	220	2,880	230	3,470	16,070
Women							
Under 25	90	-	110	2,240	-	2,440	15,330
25-29	90	-	120	1,750	50	2,010	15,850
30-34	30	-	20	450	60	560	16,660
35-39	30	-	20	270	40	360	16,720
40-49	30	-	10	250	60	350	17,260
50 and over	-	-	-	20	-	40	18,250
All ages	270	10	270	4,990	220	5,760	15,860
Men and Women	410	20	490	7,870	440	9,230	15,940
Nursery, primary and secondary schools							
Men	170	20	290	3,970	270	4,710	16,000
Women	510	30	600	12,740	420	14,310	15,760
Men and Women	680	50	890	16,710	680	19,010	15,820

Source: Database of Teacher Records.

1. Some teachers classed as new entrants by the DTR may have experience outside the scope of the Teachers Pension Scheme. This may explain the higher average salaries for older teachers.

2. Provisional data. Includes some teachers projected as entering full-time service, but whose salary is not known and hence excluded from the average salary calculation.

NEW ENTRANTS TO TEACHING

Government Office region of service of new entrants[1] to full-time teaching in maintained nursery, primary and secondary schools by sex and age, March 1999[2]

ENGLAND AND WALES

	North East	North West	Yorkshire and The Humber	East Midlands	West Midlands	East of England	London	South East	South West	England	Wales	England and Wales
Men												
Under 25	80	210	130	130	200	190	180	300	120	1,530	120	1,650
25-29	80	210	120	120	180	200	320	280	130	1,630	100	1,730
30-34	40	90	70	50	80	70	140	110	60	710	40	750
35-39	30	50	40	40	40	40	90	60	40	420	20	440
40-49	20	40	30	30	50	50	60	60	50	370	20	380
50-59	-	10	-	-	-	10	10	10	10	50	-	50
60 and over	-	-	-	-	-	-	-	-	-	-	-	-
All ages	240	600	400	360	560	560	790	810	390	4,710	300	5,010
Women												
Under 25	370	880	620	640	790	810	1,110	1,230	550	7,010	430	7,440
25-29	160	450	340	290	410	400	900	640	330	3,900	210	4,110
30-34	60	160	120	80	120	110	280	180	100	1,210	50	1,260
35-39	80	130	90	80	130	120	190	180	80	1,070	50	1,110
40-49	40	110	70	80	100	140	190	210	90	1,040	30	1,080
50-59	-	10	-	-	10	10	20	10	10	80	-	80
60 and over	-	-	-	-	-	-	-	-	-	-	-	-
All ages	720	1,740	1,240	1,170	1,550	1,590	2,680	2,460	1,160	14,310	770	15,080
Men and women												
Under 25	450	1,090	760	770	990	1,000	1,290	1,530	670	8,540	550	9,090
25-29	230	660	460	400	590	590	1,220	920	460	5,530	310	5,840
30-34	100	250	190	130	200	180	420	290	160	1,920	90	2,010
35-39	100	180	120	120	160	160	280	250	110	1,480	70	1,550
40-49	60	150	110	110	150	190	250	270	140	1,410	50	1,460
50-59	10	10	10	-	10	20	30	20	10	130	-	130
60 and over	-	-	-	-	-	-	-	-	-	-	-	-
All ages	950	2,340	1,640	1,530	2,110	2,150	3,480	3,270	1,560	19,010	1,070	20,080

Source: Database of Teacher Records.

1. Some teachers classed as new entrants by the DTR may have experience outside the scope of the Teachers Pension Scheme.
2. Provisional data.

11a(i)

TEACHER FLOWS (inflow)
Maintained nursery, primary and secondary schools: full-time teacher movement by age,[1] sector, sex and type of flow, 1998-99

ENGLAND AND WALES

	Under 25	25-29	30-34	35-39	40-44	45-49	50-54	55-59	60 and over	Total
Nursery and Primary										
Men										
New Entrants	500	400	200	100	100	-	-	-	-	1,300
Re-entrants[2]	-	100	100	100	100	100	100	-	-	600
Transfers in	-	-	-	-	-	-	-	-	-	100
Total inflow[3]	500	500	300	200	200	100	100	-	-	2,000
Women										
New Entrants	4,800	2,000	700	700	600	200	-	-	-	9,000
Re-entrants[2]	100	700	800	800	1,300	1,300	600	200	-	5,900
Transfers in	-	100	-	-	-	100	-	-	-	300
Total inflow[3]	5,000	2,800	1,500	1,600	1,900	1,500	700	200	-	15,100
Men and women										
New Entrants	5,300	2,400	900	900	600	200	-	-	-	10,300
Re-entrants[2]	100	800	900	900	1,400	1,400	700	200	-	6,400
Transfers in	-	100	-	100	100	100	-	-	-	400
Total inflow[3]	5,500	3,300	1,800	1,800	2,100	1,700	800	200	-	17,100
Secondary										
Men										
New Entrants	1,200	1,300	600	300	200	100	-	-	-	3,700
Re-entrants[2]	-	200	200	200	200	300	200	100	-	1,400
Transfers in	-	-	100	-	-	100	-	-	-	300
Total inflow[3]	1,200	1,500	900	600	500	400	300	100	-	5,400
Women										
New Entrants	2,600	2,100	600	400	300	100	-	-	-	6,100
Re-entrants[2]	-	500	500	500	800	800	400	100	-	3,500
Transfers in	-	100	100	100	100	100	100	-	-	500
Total inflow[3]	2,700	2,600	1,100	900	1,100	1,000	500	100	-	10,100
Men and women										
New Entrants	3,800	3,400	1,100	700	400	200	100	-	-	9,700
Re-entrants[2]	100	700	700	700	1,000	1,000	500	200	-	5,000
Transfers in	-	100	100	100	100	200	100	-	-	800
Total inflow[3]	3,800	4,200	2,000	1,500	1,600	1,400	700	200	-	15,500

Source: Database of Teacher Records.

1. Age as at 31 March 1999.
2 A re-entrant is defined as a teacher with some service but who was out of service at 31 March of the previous year.
3. Inflow is defined as entrants, re-entrants and transfers from other sectors.

11a(ii)

TEACHER FLOWS (outflow)

Maintained nursery, primary and secondary schools: full-time teacher movement and age by sex and type of flow, 1998-99, and age[1] by sex and sector transferred to, 1998-99

ENGLAND AND WALES

	Under 25	25-29	30-34	35-39	40-44	45-49	50-54	55-59	60 and over	Total
Men										
Transfers from full-time MNPS to:										
full-time in special schools	-	-	-	-	-	-	-	-	-	200
full-time in further and higher education[2]	-	-	-	-	-	-	-	-	-	100
full-time other sectors	-	100	100	100	100	100	-	-	-	500
All transfers out	-	100	100	100	100	100	100	-	-	700
Other leavers incl to part-time	100	900	800	600	600	1,100	1,500	700	600	6,900
Total wastage[3]	100	1,000	900	700	800	1,300	1,500	700	600	7,600
Women										
Transfers from full-time MNPS to:										
full-time in special schools	-	100	100	100	100	100	-	-	-	400
full-time in further and higher education[2]	-	-	-	-	-	-	-	-	-	100
full-time other sectors	-	300	200	100	100	200	100	-	-	1,000
All transfers out	-	400	200	200	200	300	200	-	-	1,600
Other leavers incl to part-time	500	3,700	3,600	2,100	2,100	2,800	2,800	1,500	1,500	20,700
Total wastage[3]	500	4,100	3,800	2,200	2,300	3,100	3,000	1,600	1,500	22,200
Men and women										
Transfers from full-time MNPS to:										
full-time in special schools	-	100	100	100	100	100	100	-	-	600
full-time in further and higher education[2]	-	-	-	-	-	100	-	-	-	300
full-time other sectors	-	400	200	200	200	200	200	-	-	1,500
All transfers out	100	500	400	300	300	400	200	-	-	2,300
Other leavers incl to part-time	500	4,600	4,300	2,700	2,800	4,000	4,300	2,200	2,200	27,500
Total wastage[3]	600	5,100	4,700	3,000	3,100	4,300	4,500	2,300	2,200	29,800

Source: Database of Teacher Records.

1. Age as at 31 March 1999.
2. Including further education for adults.
3. Wastage is teachers leaving full-time service in the maintained nursery, primary and secondary sector during the year, some of whom may continue in part-time service or in a different sector.

TEACHER FLOWS
Maintained nursery, primary and secondary schools: 1988-89, 1993-94, 1997-98 and 1998-99; teacher movement by type and destination

ENGLAND AND WALES

	1988-89	1993-94	1997-98	1998-99[1]	1998-99 England only[1]
Entrants to full-time teaching in the maintained nursery, primary and secondary sector					
New entrants to teaching	13,600	17,600	21,600	20,100	19,000
Those who in previous March were:					
full-time service other sector	1,400	1,000	1,300	1,200	1,100
part-time service in any sector	5,300	5,000	5,400	4,900	4,700
other service (mainly occasional)	1,300	800	900	800	800
out of service	8,500	6,500	5,400	5,400	5,000
previously retired	100	200	200	200	200
other[2]	-	-	-	-	.
total	16,600	13,500	13,100	12,500	11,800
Total entrants	30,200	31,100	34,700	32,600	30,800
Movement from full-time teaching in the maintained nursery, primary and secondary sector					
Those who moved to:					
full-time service other sector	3,400	1,900	2,000	2,300	2,200
part-time service in any sector	4,300	5,600	7,300	7,000	6,700
other service (mainly occasional)	1,100	800	1,100	1,400	1,300
out of service	14,500	10,800	12,400	12,800	12,200
retirement	12,600	12,800	14,500	5,800	5,400
other[2]	1,100	500	400	500	500
total	36,900	32,300	37,700	29,800	28,300
Entrants to part-time teaching in the maintained nursery, primary and secondary sector					
New entrants to teaching	800	1,300	1,500	1,300	1,200
Those who in previous March were:					
part-time service other sector	200	200	900	1,100	1,000
full-time service any sector	4,300	5,400	7,000	6,600	6,300
other service (mainly occasional)	1,100	1,000	1,000	1,000	900
out of service	8,500	5,900	4,000	3,600	3,500
previously retired	400	900	1,200	1,200	1,200
other[2]	-	-	-	-	-
total	14,400	13,500	14,000	13,600	13,000
Total entrants	15,200	14,800	15,500	14,900	14,200
Movement from part-time teaching in the maintained nursery, primary and secondary sector					
Those who moved to:					
full-time service any sector	5,400	4,900	5,100	4,800	4,500
part-time service other sector	300	800	1,200	1,300	1,300
other service (mainly occasional)	800	800	1,100	1,200	1,100
out of service	5,400	5,000	4,300	3,800	3,600
retirement	700	1,700	2,800	2,400	2,300
other[2]	100	100	-	100	100
total	12,700	13,300	14,600	13,400	12,900

Source: Database of Teacher Records.

1. Provisional estimates.
2. Including those whose position is not known.

11b(i)

TEACHER FLOWS (inflow)
Maintained nursery, primary and secondary schools: full-time teacher movement by age,[1] sector, sex and type of flow, 1998-99

ENGLAND ONLY

	Under 25	25-29	30-34	35-39	40-44	45-49	50-54	55-59	60 and over	Total
Nursery and Primary										
Men										
New Entrants	500	400	200	100	100	-	-	-	-	1,200
Re-entrants[2]	-	100	100	100	100	100	100	-	-	500
Transfers in	-	-	-	-	-	-	-	-	-	100
Total inflow[3]	500	500	300	200	200	100	100	-	-	1,800
Women										
New Entrants	4,600	1,900	700	700	500	200	-	-	-	8,600
Re-entrants[2]	100	600	700	700	1,200	1,200	600	200	-	5,400
Transfers in	-	-	-	-	-	100	-	-	-	300
Total inflow[3]	4,700	2,600	1,400	1,500	1,800	1,500	600	200	-	14,300
Men and women										
New Entrants	5,000	2,300	800	800	600	200	-	-	-	9,800
Re-entrants[2]	100	700	800	800	1,300	1,300	700	200	-	6,000
Transfers in	-	100	-	-	100	100	-	-	-	300
Total inflow[3]	5,100	3,100	1,700	1,700	2,000	1,600	700	200	-	16,100
Secondary										
Men										
New Entrants	1,100	1,200	500	300	200	100	-	-	-	3,500
Re-entrants[2]	-	200	200	200	200	200	200	100	-	1,400
Transfers in	-	-	100	-	-	100	-	-	-	300
Total inflow[3]	1,100	1,500	800	500	400	400	300	100	-	5,100
Women										
New Entrants	2,400	2,000	600	400	200	100	-	-	-	5,800
Re-entrants[2]	-	400	500	500	700	700	300	100	-	3,300
Transfers in	-	100	100	100	100	100	100	-	-	500
Total inflow[3]	2,500	2,500	1,100	900	1,100	1,000	400	100	-	9,600
Men and women										
New Entrants	3,500	3,200	1,100	700	400	200	100	-	-	9,200
Re-entrants[2]	100	600	700	700	1,000	1,000	500	200	-	4,700
Transfers in	-	100	100	100	100	200	100	-	-	800
Total inflow[3]	3,600	4,000	1,900	1,400	1,500	1,400	700	200	-	14,700

Source: Database of Teacher Records.

1. Age as at 31 March 1999.
2. A re-entrant is defined as a teacher with some service but who was out of service at 31 March of the previous year.
3. Inflow is defined as entrants, re-entrants and transfers from other sectors.

TEACHER FLOWS (outflow)

Maintained nursery, primary and secondary schools: full-time teacher movement and age by sex and type of flow, 1998-99, and age[1] by sex and sector transferred to, 1998-99

ENGLAND ONLY

	Under 25	25-29	30-34	35-39	40-44	45-49	50-54	55-59	60 and over	Total
Men										
Transfers from full-time MNPS to:										
full-time in special schools	-	-	-	-	-	-	-	-	-	100
full-time in further and higher education[2]	-	-	-	-	-	-	-	-	-	100
Other sectors	-	100	100	100	100	100	-	-	-	400
All transfers out	-	100	100	100	100	100	100	-	-	700
Other leavers incl to part-time	100	800	700	600	600	1,100	1,400	600	600	6,500
Total wastage[3]	100	1,000	900	700	700	1,200	1,400	600	600	7,200
Women										
Transfers from full-time MNPS to:										
full-time in special schools	-	100	100	-	100	100	-	-	-	400
full-time in further and higher education[2]	-	-	-	-	-	-	-	-	-	100
Other sectors	-	300	100	100	100	200	100	-	-	1,000
All transfers out	-	400	200	200	200	300	200	-	-	1,500
Other leavers incl to part-time	400	3,600	3,400	2,000	2,000	2,700	2,700	1,500	1,500	19,600
Total wastage[3]	500	3,900	3,600	2,100	2,200	2,900	2,800	1,500	1,500	21,100
Men and women										
Transfers from full-time MNPS to:										
full-time in special schools	-	100	100	100	100	100	100	-	-	500
full-time in further and higher education[2]	-	-	-	-	-	-	-	-	-	200
Other sectors	-	400	200	200	200	200	100	-	-	1,400
All transfers out	100	500	400	300	300	400	200	-	-	2,200
Other leavers incl to part-time	500	4,400	4,100	2,600	2,600	3,700	4,000	2,100	2,100	26,100
Total wastage[3]	600	4,900	4,500	2,800	3,000	4,100	4,300	2,100	2,100	28,300

Source: Database of Teacher Records.

1. Age as at 31 March 1999.
2. Including further education for adults.
3. Wastage is teachers leaving full-time service in the maintained nursery, primary and secondary sector during the year, some of whom may continue in part-time service or in a different sector.

12

TEACHER FLOWS

Turnover and wastage rates by government office region, 1997-98[1]

ENGLAND AND WALES   (percentages)

Government office region	Turnover rate[2]	Wastage rate[3]
North East	14.2	9.0
North West	14.9	9.0
Yorkshire and The Humber	15.5	9.2
East Midlands[2]	13.8	8.5
West Midlands	14.6	8.9
East of England	16.0	9.7
London	19.3	11.7
Of which :		
Inner London	21.0	12.9
Outer London	18.5	11.0
South East	16.9	10.5
South West	15.5	10.4
England	15.9	9.8
Wales	14.6	9.8
England and Wales	15.8	9.8

Source: Database of Teacher Records.

1. Data are provisional.
2. Turnover is defined as all teachers in full-time service in the maintained nursery, primary and secondary schools sector on 31 March 1997 who were not in full-time service in the same establishment on 31 March 1998 (where a teacher moves from a school with a local education authority maintained establishment number to a school with a grant-maintained establishment number within the same local authority, it is assumed that the teacher is in the same school but that it has changed to grant-maintained status). Turnover therefore includes both wastage and transfers to other establishments within the maintained nursery, primary and secondary sector. Turnover based on data excluding one local authority because of unusually high turnover caused by technical reasons.
3. Wastage is defined as all teachers in full-time service in the maintained nursery, primary and secondary sector on 31 March 1997 who were not in full-time service anywhere in that sector on 31 March 1998.

TEACHER FLOWS
Teacher[1] movement by government office region, 1997 to 1998

ENGLAND AND WALES

	Total full-time teachers March 1997	All leaving full-time service [2]	Total Entrants [3]	Movement between regions [4]	Total full-time teachers March 1998
England	345,980	34,960	32,140	-30	343,120
North East	19,920	1,830	1,610	-20	19,670
North West	52,970	4,860	4,470	10	52,590
Yorkshire and The Humber	36,670	3,530	3,020	60	36,220
East Midlands	29,080	2,850	2,270	-	28,490
West Midlands	40,560	3,690	3,350	20	40,240
East of England	37,360	3,690	3,810	-10	37,470
London	46,790	5,700	5,330	-470	45,950
South East	51,250	5,430	5,240	110	51,180
South West	31,390	3,380	3,040	260	31,310
Wales	24,560	2,570	1,990	30	24,010
England and Wales	370,540	37,530	34,130	-	367,130

Source: Database of Teacher Records.

1. Full time teachers in maintained nursery, primary and secondary schools. Excludes those whose region of service is not known.
2. Includes teachers moving to part-time teaching, other sectors and retirements.
3. Includes entrant and re-entrants to full-time teaching.
4. Net imports (positive numbers) indicate inflow of full-time teachers from other regions, net exports (negative numbers) indicate an outflow.

TEACHERS IN SERVICE

14

Teacher numbers: 1995 to 2000 by sector and type of contract

ENGLAND AND WALES

	January						2000 (England only)
	1995	1996	1997	1998	1999	2000	
Nursery and primary							
Qualified teachers	211,000	212,160	212,530	210,630	212,590	216,170	202,160
Full-time							
In regular service	188,010	188,490	188,050	185,950	186,200	187,110	174,720
On secondment [1]	100	160	130	100	140	180	170
In occasional service	8,040	8,280	8,880	8,900	9,580	11,340	10,520
FTE of part-time	14,840	15,240	15,470	15,690	16,680	17,550	16,750
Teachers without QTS [2]	1,050	1,080	1,010	1,140	1,240	1,490	1,460
Total teachers	212,040	213,240	213,540	211,780	213,830	217,660	203,620
Secondary							
Qualified teachers	205,610	205,280	205,390	204,680	207,590	209,450	196,420
Full-time							
In regular service	187,510	186,720	186,590	185,830	187,900	188,420	176,520
On secondment [1]	60	50	50	40	40	120	110
In occasional service	4,660	4,630	4,840	4,430	4,940	5,880	5,320
FTE of part-time	13,380	13,870	13,920	14,380	14,710	15,030	14,460
Teachers without QTS [2]	2,180	1,860	1,830	1,920	2,100	2,120	2,100
Total teachers	207,780	207,140	207,220	206,600	209,690	211,570	198,520
Special schools							
Qualified teachers	16,260	16,100	15,990	15,500	15,400	15,430	14,810
Full-time							
In regular service	14,520	14,290	14,040	13,570	13,420	13,350	12,810
On secondment [1]	30	40	30	10	10	30	30
In occasional service	630	650	700	700	690	720	690
FTE of part-time	1,070	1,130	1,220	1,220	1,270	1,320	1,280
Teachers without QTS [2]	310	180	150	170	230	210	210
Total teachers	16,560	16,280	16,140	15,670	15,620	15,640	15,020
Education elsewhere [3]							
Qualified teachers	2,980	3,510	3,660	3,900	4,100	4,260	4,100
Full-time							
In regular service	2,340	2,640	2,700	2,900	3,170	3,220	3,100
On secondment [1]	10	10	-	10	-	-	-
In occasional service	80	180	230	220	100	150	140
FTE of part-time	560	680	730	770	820	890	860
Teachers without QTS [2]	20	10	10	30	30	40	40
Total teachers	3,000	3,520	3,680	3,930	4,130	4,300	4,140
Total [3]	439,380	440,100	440,580	437,980	443,280	449,180	421,300

Source: DfEE annual 618G survey and National Assembly for Wales stats3 survey.

1. For periods of one term or more.
2. Teachers without Qualified Teacher Status, full-time and FTE of part-time.
3. Includes Pupil Referral Units.

15

TEACHERS IN SERVICE
Full-time teachers in maintained secondary schools – teaching-contact ratios[1] by type of teacher

ENGLAND

	Timetabled teaching as percentage of timetabled week
Type of teacher:	
Head teacher	16
Deputy head	38
Other qualified teacher	76
Unqualified teacher	73
Full-time teachers	74
Full-time teachers (excluding head teachers and deputy head teachers)	76

Source : 1996/97 Secondary Schools Curriculum and Staffing Survey

1. Restricted to teachers teaching at least one period a week.

16

Full-time equivalent[1] teacher numbers 2000: by sector and government office region

ENGLAND AND WALES

Government office region:	Nursery and primary [2]	Secondary [2]	Special	Elsewhere	Total
North East	10,900	11,050	870	280	23,110
North West	30,540	28,990	2,470	590	62,590
Yorkshire and The Humber	21,760	21,130	1,410	380	44,680
East Midlands	16,700	17,370	1,040	300	35,410
West Midlands	22,770	22,710	1,910	530	47,930
East of England	21,070	22,410	1,370	320	45,170
London	30,600	26,390	2,330	760	60,080
South East	30,570	29,900	2,400	610	63,480
South West	18,700	18,570	1,210	360	38,850
England	203,620	198,520	15,020	4,140	421,300
Wales	14,040	13,050	620	160	27,880
England and Wales	217,660	211,570	15,640	4,300	449,180

Source: DfEE annual 618G survey and National Assembly for Wales stats3 survey.

1. Part-time teachers have been converted to an estimate of their full-time equivalency and added to full-time numbers.
2. Teachers whose service is divided between primary and secondary schools have been apportioned pro-rata to the nursery/ primary or secondary phase.

TEACHERS IN SERVICE
Teacher numbers in maintained nursery, primary and secondary schools[1]: type of contract by LEA and Government Office region, 2000

ENGLAND AND WALES

	Qualified regular [2] full-time & secondments	Qualified regular [2] part-time FTE	Occasional teachers		Teachers without QTS [3]	Total FTE
			Agency	Occasional		
Gateshead	1,470	70	-	90	10	1,640
Newcastle upon Tyne	1,920	110	50	10	10	2,110
North Tyneside	1,430	90	40	50	-	1,610
South Tyneside	1,190	40	20	40	-	1,290
Sunderland	2,390	70	-	80	10	2,550
Hartlepool	760	20	10	30	10	830
Middlesbrough	1,150	50	10	30	10	1,250
Redcar and Cleveland	1,190	60	10	40	10	1,300
Stockton on Tees	1,510	70	-	90	10	1,680
Durham	3,840	150	70	190	20	4,270
Darlington	730	30	-	30	-	800
Northumberland	2,240	250	-	120	-	2,620
North East	**19,820**	**1,020**	**220**	**800**	**100**	**21,950**
Bolton	2,300	100	20	90	10	2,520
Bury	1,340	70	-	70	-	1,490
Manchester	3,240	170	-	120	50	3,580
Oldham	2,010	110	-	40	10	2,160
Rochdale	1,700	100	30	70	10	1,910
Salford	1,800	30	40	40	10	1,910
Stockport	1,940	140	20	40	-	2,140
Tameside	1,780	80	30	50	10	1,950
Trafford	1,730	100	-	10	-	1,850
Wigan	2,420	120	60	90	-	2,700
Cheshire	5,000	410	-	170	30	5,600
Halton	1,040	50	10	10	-	1,110
Warrington	1,480	90	30	20	30	1,640
Lancashire	8,440	700	-	350	50	9,540
Blackburn with Darwen	1,220	90	30	40	10	1,380
Blackpool	920	60	10	50	10	1,040
Cumbria	3,660	470	-	160	20	4,320
Knowsley	1,450	60	50	30	-	1,580
Liverpool	3,690	160	100	70	20	4,040
St Helens	1,440	50	-	60	-	1,550
Sefton	2,300	130	-	140	10	2,580
Wirral	2,650	160	30	90	10	2,940
North West	**53,540**	**3,450**	**470**	**1,780**	**310**	**59,530**

17

TEACHERS IN SERVICE

Teacher numbers in maintained nursery, primary and secondary schools[1]: type of contract by LEA and Government Office region, 2000

ENGLAND AND WALES

	Qualified regular [2] full-time & secondments	Qualified regular [2] part-time FTE	Occasional teachers		Teachers without QTS [3]	Total FTE
			Agency	Occasional		
Barnsley	1,560	40	50	90	-	1,740
Doncaster	2,400	150	20	60	10	2,630
Rotherham	2,130	120	30	90	10	2,390
Sheffield	3,270	410	-	180	70	3,930
Bradford	4,070	310	-	240	40	4,650
Calderdale	1,640	110	20	80	-	1,860
Kirklees	2,920	240	10	130	20	3,310
Leeds	5,570	350	70	90	20	6,100
Wakefield	2,380	70	40	90	10	2,590
City of Kingston-upon-Hull	1,880	130	50	50	20	2,140
East Riding of Yorkshire	2,200	220	20	90	10	2,530
North East Lincolnshire	1,240	70	60	-	10	1,380
North Lincolnshire	1,150	90	10	40	10	1,300
North Yorkshire	4,210	480	20	170	30	4,910
York	1,130	150	-	130	10	1,420
Yorkshire and The Humber	**37,740**	**2,940**	**390**	**1,530**	**280**	**42,880**
Derbyshire	4,890	500	50	190	20	5,660
Derby	1,640	140	-	70	30	1,880
Leicestershire	4,250	540	40	110	50	4,980
Leicester City	2,160	240	80	50	30	2,560
Rutland	220	-	-	-	-	220
Lincolnshire	4,450	380	-	220	40	5,090
Northamptonshire	4,900	410	-	150	30	5,490
Nottinghamshire	5,270	470	-	340	-	6,090
City of Nottingham	1,820	150	70	50	10	2,100
East Midlands	**29,590**	**2,830**	**240**	**1,190**	**220**	**34,070**
Birmingham	8,540	550	210	-	60	9,360
Coventry	2,390	210	20	60	20	2,710
Dudley	2,460	130	20	100	30	2,740
Sandwell	2,370	160	30	30	10	2,600
Solihull	1,720	160	20	30	10	1,940
Walsall	2,060	210	10	60	10	2,350
Wolverhampton	2,010	120	20	40	40	2,230
Hereford	1,120	130	-	20	-	1,270
Worcester	3,640	340	-	170	10	4,160
Shropshire	1,830	170	-	100	20	2,120
Telford & Wrekin	1,160	90	10	60	-	1,330
Staffordshire	5,970	420	60	220	30	6,690
Stoke	1,720	80	40	110	10	1,950
Warwickshire	3,470	400	20	110	50	4,040
West Midlands	**40,450**	**3,190**	**450**	**1,100**	**300**	**45,490**

17

CONTINUED
TEACHERS IN SERVICE
Teacher numbers in maintained nursery, primary and secondary schools[1]: type of contract by LEA and Government Office region, 2000

ENGLAND AND WALES

	Qualified regular [2] full-time & secondments	Qualified regular [2] part-time FTE	Occasional teachers		Teachers without QTS [3]	Total FTE
			Agency	Occasional		
Cambridgeshire	3,380	370	-	60	50	3,860
Peterborough	1,450	80	-	-	10	1,540
Norfolk	5,170	460	-	260	60	5,950
Suffolk	4,760	490	-	260	50	5,560
Bedfordshire	2,870	280	20	110	30	3,310
Luton	1,450	100	-	50	60	1,660
Essex	9,220	720	90	230	130	10,390
Southend	1,140	130	10	30	30	1,330
Thurrock	980	50	20	30	20	1,100
Hertfordshire	7,610	900	80	80	100	8,770
East of England	**38,030**	**3,590**	**220**	**1,100**	**540**	**43,480**
City of London	10	-	-	-	-	20
Camden	1,080	140	80	20	30	1,350
Greenwich	1,670	210	40	10	20	1,950
Hackney	1,300	90	100	10	30	1,530
Hammersmith & Fulham	800	100	70	10	30	1,000
Islington	1,150	110	120	10	10	1,400
Kensington & Chelsea	530	50	40	10	30	650
Lambeth	1,280	170	70	10	40	1,570
Lewisham	1,540	220	70	10	20	1,870
Southwark	1,560	100	120	10	50	1,840
Tower Hamlets	1,780	210	70	10	140	2,210
Wandsworth	1,350	150	40	10	20	1,570
Westminster	1,010	80	50	-	50	1,190
Barking and Dagenham	1,340	60	40	20	30	1,480
Barnet	2,280	320	50	30	50	2,720
Bexley	1,700	120	90	40	10	1,960
Brent	1,840	140	40	70	30	2,110
Bromley	2,030	150	40	60	10	2,300
Croydon	2,340	390	70	30	30	2,860
Ealing	1,950	130	50	10	40	2,190
Enfield	2,270	260	60	30	40	2,670
Haringey	1,610	120	50	30	30	1,850
Harrow	1,140	190	80	30	30	1,460
Havering	1,640	160	50	50	40	1,930
Hillingdon	1,850	130	40	30	30	2,080
Hounslow	1,700	140	50	30	30	1,950
Kingston upon Thames	890	120	20	20	-	1,040
Merton	970	110	60	10	20	1,180
Newham	2,170	80	190	10	40	2,490
Redbridge	1,870	150	20	10	50	2,100
Richmond upon Thames	830	160	20	40	10	1,050
Sutton	1,270	140	30	30	10	1,490
Waltham Forest	1,710	130	30	20	40	1,930
London	**48,470**	**4,820**	**1,910**	**730**	**1,070**	**56,990**

17 TEACHERS IN SERVICE

Teacher numbers in maintained nursery, primary and secondary schools[1]: type of contract by LEA and Government Office region, 2000

ENGLAND AND WALES

	Qualified regular [2] full-time & secondments	Qualified regular [2] part-time FTE	Occasional teachers		Teachers without QTS [3]	Total FTE
			Agency	Occasional		
Bracknell Forest	650	80	20	30	-	790
Windsor & Maidenhead	840	100	20	-	30	990
West Berkshire	1,250	120	-	30	10	1,400
Reading	800	60	-	20	-	880
Slough	870	80	40	10	30	1,030
Wokingham	1,050	110	-	-	-	1,170
Buckinghamshire	3,190	460	-	30	40	3,730
Milton Keynes	1,540	110	10	70	30	1,760
East Sussex	3,010	350	30	80	20	3,490
Brighton & Hove	1,350	170	10	40	20	1,580
Hampshire	7,700	860	70	330	50	9,020
Portsmouth	1,250	70	30	40	20	1,410
Southampton	1,420	120	40	40	-	1,620
Isle of Wight	930	90	-	30	10	1,050
Kent	9,690	960	100	330	130	11,210
Medway	1,880	180	30	30	50	2,160
Oxfordshire	3,860	490	10	110	60	4,530
Surrey	6,180	790	60	110	30	7,170
West Sussex	4,720	590	30	110	30	5,480
South East	**52,180**	**5,810**	**480**	**1,440**	**560**	**60,470**
Isles of Scilly	20	-	-	-	-	20
Bath & NE Somerset	1,170	140	10	50	-	1,370
City of Bristol	2,270	250	50	140	20	2,740
North Somerset	1,190	110	-	90	-	1,390
South Gloucestershire	1,800	230	20	60	-	2,110
Cornwall	3,280	310	-	260	30	3,880
Devon	4,240	540	-	260	20	5,050
Plymouth	1,880	150	10	90	20	2,140
Torbay	770	100	10	30	-	910
Dorset	2,420	260	-	90	20	2,800
Poole	890	70	-	30	10	990
Bournemouth	930	100	10	30	10	1,080
Gloucestershire	3,850	530	-	150	10	4,540
Somerset	3,050	340	10	210	30	3,630
Wiltshire	2,670	330	20	110	20	3,140
Swindon	1,310	110	20	40	10	1,480
South West	**31,720**	**3,560**	**160**	**1,640**	**190**	**37,270**
England	**351,530**	**31,210**	**4,540**	**11,290**	**3,560**	**402,140**

TEACHERS IN SERVICE

Teacher numbers in maintained nursery, primary and secondary schools[1]: type of contract by LEA and Government Office region, 2000

17

ENGLAND AND WALES

	Qualified regular [2] full-time & secondments	Qualified regular [2] part-time FTE	Occasional teachers		Teachers without QTS [3]	Total FTE
			Agency	Occasional		
Isle of Anglesey	550	30	-	50	-	630
Gwynedd	960	90	-	80	-	1,130
Conwy	810	50	-	20	-	890
Denbighshire	720	50	-	40	-	810
Flintshire	1,150	100	-	120	-	1,370
Wrexham	840	80	-	200	-	1,120
Powys	1,060	80	-	110	10	1,260
Ceredigion	600	30	-	30	-	670
Pembrokeshire	1,030	60	-	110	-	1,200
Carmarthenshire	1,490	110	-	160	-	1,760
Swansea	1,810	100	-	-	-	1,900
Neath Port Talbot	1,210	70	-	60	-	1,350
Bridgend	1,160	20	-	40	-	1,220
Vale of Glamorgan	880	50	-	60	-	990
Rhondda Cynon Taff	2,230	50	-	10	-	2,290
Merthyr Tydfil	570	30	-	10	-	610
Caerphilly	1,470	60	-	40	10	1,570
Blaenau Gwent	610	20	-	20	-	640
Torfaen	810	30	-	30	-	870
Monmouthshire	600	30	-	80	-	710
Newport	1,280	50	-	80	-	1,410
Cardiff	2,470	170	-	50	-	2,700
Wales	**24,300**	**1,370**	**-**	**1,380**	**40**	**27,090**
England and Wales	**375,830**	**32,580**	**4,540**	**12,680**	**3,610**	**429,230**

Source: DfEE annual 618G survey and National Assembly for Wales annual stats3 survey.

1. Excludes sixth form colleges.
2. Includes regular supply teachers.
3. Teachers without Qualified Teacher Status.

TEACHERS IN SERVICE
Teacher numbers: type of contract and country by sector, 2000

ENGLAND AND WALES

	England and Wales				Wales	England
	Qualified regular [1] full-time	Qualified regular [1] part-time (fte)	Others [2]	Total		
Nursery and primary	182,970	16,200	12,560	211,730	13,620	198,100
Secondary	184,400	13,720	7,560	205,680	12,640	193,030
Miscellaneous primary and secondary [3]	8,160	2,670	1,000	11,830	830	11,000
Special [4]	13,350	1,320	970	15,640	620	15,020
Not in schools [5]	3,220	890	190	4,300	160	4,140
Total	392,100	34,790	22,280	449,180	27,880	421,300

Source: DfEE annual 618G survey and National Assembly for Wales stats3 survey.

1. Includes regular supply teachers.
2. Qualified teachers in occasional service or on secondment for one term or more, plus instructors and teachers on routes to Qualified Teacher Status.
3. Teachers whose service is divided between primary and secondary, peripatetic and advisory teachers and teachers in miscellaneous primary and secondary establishments.
4. Excluding non-maintained special schools.
5. Includes those teaching in pupil referral units and those employed by local education authorities but not teaching in schools or primary and secondary establishments, e.g. home tuition services.

19 TEACHERS IN SERVICE
Part-time qualified teachers in maintained nursery, primary, secondary [1] and special [2] schools: 1985 to 2000

ENGLAND AND WALES

| | Part-time teachers (thousands) | | |
	Number	Full-time equivalent (FTE)	FTE as % of total teaching force
1985	35.8	16.1	3.6
1990	52.0	24.0	5.5
1991	54.1	25.3	5.8
1992	57.2	27.0	6.2
1993	58.3	27.5	6.3
1994 [3]	59.7	28.0	6.5
1995 [3]	61.9	29.3	6.8
1996 [3]	63.8	30.2	6.9
1997 [3]	64.2	30.6	7.0
1998 [3]	65.3	31.3	7.2
1999 [3]	67.0	32.7	7.4
2000 [3]	68.9	33.9	7.6
Of which:			
Nursery and primary [1]	37.4	17.5	7.3
Secondary [1]	28.9	15.0	6.7
Special [2]	2.5	1.3	6.6
England only			
2000 [3]	65.9	32.5	7.8
Of which:			
Nursery and primary [1]	35.7	16.7	8.1
Secondary [1]	27.8	14.5	7.1
Special [2]	2.5	1.3	7.2

Source: DfEE annual 618G survey and National Assembly for Wales stats3 survey.

1. Teachers whose service is divided between primary and secondary schools, peripatetic teachers and teachers in remedial centres or other establishments are apportioned to nursery and primary or secondary schools.
2. Teachers in pupil referral units or unattached special units are not included in the figures for special schools.
3. Sixth form colleges are excluded from 1994 onwards.

TEACHERS IN SERVICE
FTE teacher numbers: 1995 to 2000 by country and sector

ENGLAND AND WALES

	1995	1996	1997	1998	1999	2000
England						
Nursery, primary and secondary[1]	392,910	393,330	393,800	391,970	396,280	402,140
Special[2] and education not in schools[3]	18,920	19,060	18,990	18,840	19,010	19,160
Total	411,830	412,400	412,790	410,810	415,290	421,300
Wales						
Nursery, primary and secondary[1]	26,910	26,970	26,960	26,410	27,240	27,100
Special[2] and education not in schools[3]	730	740	830	760	750	780
Total	27,640	27,710	27,790	27,170	27,990	27,880
England and Wales						
Nursery, primary and secondary[1]	419,820	420,380	420,760	418,380	423,520	429,230
Special[2] and education not in schools[3]	19,560	19,800	19,820	19,600	19,770	19,940
Total	439,380	440,100	440,580	437,980	443,280	449,180

Source: DfEE annual 618G survey and National Assembly for Wales stats3 survey.

1. Sixth form colleges are excluded.
2. Excluding non-maintained special schools, but including grant-maintained and foundation special schools.
3. Includes those teaching in pupil referral units and those employed by local education authorities but not teaching in schools or primary and secondary establishments, e.g. home tuition services.

TEACHERS IN SERVICE
Full-time teachers in maintained nursery/primary, secondary [1] and special schools: 1995-1999 by sector, grade and sex

ENGLAND AND WALES

	1995		1996		1997		1998		1999 [2]		England only 1999 [2]	
	Numbers (000s)	%	Numbers (000s)	%	Numbers (000s)	%	Numbers (000s)	%	Numbers (000s)	%	Numbers (000s)	%
Nursery and primary												
Heads												
Men	10.0	47.7	9.8	46.6	9.3	44.8	8.8	42.8	8.4	41.5	7.6	41.0
Women	11.0	52.3	11.2	53.4	11.5	55.2	11.8	57.2	11.8	58.5	10.9	59.0
All teachers	21.0	100	21.1	100	20.8	100	20.6	100	20.2	100	18.5	100
Deputy heads												
Men	5.4	30.6	5.1	29.6	4.8	28.7	4.4	27.4	4.4	27.2	4.0	27.0
Women	12.2	69.4	12.1	70.4	11.9	71.3	11.7	72.6	11.7	72.8	10.8	73.0
All teachers	17.7	100	17.2	100	16.6	100	16.1	100	16.1	100	14.8	100
Classroom and others [3]												
Men	16.9	11.8	17.0	11.8	17.0	11.8	16.9	11.8	17.2	11.8	16.1	11.9
Women	126.1	88.2	126.8	88.2	127.3	88.2	126.4	88.2	127.8	88.2	119.7	88.1
All teachers	143.0	100	143.8	100	144.3	100	143.3	100	145.0	100	135.7	100
All teachers												
Men	32.3	17.8	31.9	17.5	31.1	17.1	30.1	16.7	29.9	16.5	27.7	16.4
Women	149.4	82.2	150.1	82.5	150.6	82.9	150.0	83.3	151.3	83.5	141.4	83.6
All teachers	181.7	100	182.0	100	181.7	100	180.1	100	181.3	100	169.1	100
Secondary												
Heads												
Men	3.4	76.4	3.3	75.8	3.3	74.9	3.2	73.1	3.1	72.2	2.9	71.5
Women	1.0	23.6	1.1	24.2	1.1	25.1	1.2	26.9	1.2	27.8	1.2	28.5
All teachers	4.4	100	4.4	100	4.3	100	4.3	100	4.3	100	4.0	100
Deputy heads												
Men	5.3	66.1	5.0	65.5	4.6	65.1	4.5	64.9	4.4	64.3	4.1	63.9
Women	2.7	33.9	2.6	34.5	2.5	34.9	2.4	35.1	2.5	35.7	2.3	36.1
All teachers	8.1	100	7.6	100	7.1	100	6.9	100	6.9	100	6.4	100
Classroom and others [3]												
Men	84.6	47.5	83.3	47.0	82.3	46.4	80.6	45.7	80.6	45.3	75.5	45.3
Women	93.5	52.5	93.9	53.0	95.3	53.7	95.9	54.3	97.5	54.7	91.1	54.7
All teachers	178.1	100	177.1	100	177.5	100	176.4	100	178.1	100	166.6	100
All teachers												
Men	93.3	49.0	91.5	48.4	90.1	47.7	88.2	47.0	88.1	46.6	82.5	46.6
Women	97.2	51.0	97.6	51.6	98.9	52.3	99.4	53.0	101.1	53.4	94.5	53.4
All teachers	190.6	100	189.1	100	189.0	100	187.7	100	189.3	100	177.1	100

TEACHERS IN SERVICE

23

Full-time teachers in maintained nursery, primary and secondary schools: 1985 to 1999 by sex and type of school

ENGLAND AND WALES

	1985	1990	1995	1996	1997	1998	1999 [1]	1999 [1] England only
Men								
Nursery	10	20	40	50	40	40	40	40
Primary [2]								
Grant-maintained	.	.	790	870	940	970	960	950
LEA Maintained	37,570	34,600	31,470	30,970	30,070	29,100	28,950	26,700
All primary schools	37,570	34,600	32,260	31,850	31,010	30,070	29,910	27,650
Secondary [3]								
Grant-maintained	.	500	16,350	16,740	17,210	17,250	17,270	16,990
LEA Maintained	127,010	105,970	76,350	74,140	72,280	70,400	70,310	65,000
All secondary schools	127,010	106,470	92,700	90,880	89,490	87,650	87,580	81,990
Divided service [4]	630	880	610	630	590	550	540	520
Miscellaneous	200	80	30	20	20	20	20	20
All nursery, primary and secondary	165,420	142,040	125,640	123,430	121,160	118,330	118,080	110,220
Women								
Nursery	1,680	1,590	1,490	1,470	1,450	1,390	1,360	1,270
Primary [2]								
Grant-maintained	.	.	3,530	3,930	4,260	4,450	4,540	4,490
LEA Maintained	132,100	142,530	144,340	144,740	144,920	144,120	145,430	135,640
All primary schools	132,100	142,530	147,870	148,670	149,180	148,570	149,970	140,140
Secondary [3]								
Grant-maintained	.	310	15,620	16,450	17,210	17,850	18,110	17,780
LEA Maintained	107,690	97,160	80,250	79,720	80,370	80,410	81,820	75,600
All secondary schools	107,690	97,470	95,870	96,170	97,580	98,260	99,930	93,370
Divided service [4]	1,140	1,460	1,310	1,320	1,230	1,120	1,120	1,100
Miscellaneous	180	90	60	80	70	60	60	60
All nursery, primary and secondary	242,790	243,130	246,600	247,700	249,500	249,400	252,440	235,930
Men and Women								
Nursery	1,690	1,610	1,530	1,520	1,490	1,430	1,400	1,310
Primary [2]								
Grant-maintained	-	-	4,320	4,810	5,200	5,420	5,500	5,440
LEA Maintained	169,680	177,120	175,800	175,710	174,990	173,220	174,380	162,340
All primary schools	169,680	177,120	180,130	180,520	180,190	178,640	179,870	167,780
Secondary [3]								
Grant-maintained	-	810	31,970	33,190	34,420	35,100	35,380	34,770
LEA Maintained	234,700	203,130	156,610	153,860	152,650	150,820	152,130	140,590
All secondary schools	234,700	203,930	188,580	187,050	187,070	185,920	187,510	175,360
Divided service [4]	1,780	2,340	1,910	1,950	1,820	1,660	1,660	1,620
Miscellaneous	380	170	90	100	90	80	80	80
All nursery, primary and secondary	408,210	385,180	372,240	371,130	370,660	367,730	370,530	346,150

Source: Database of Teacher Records.

1. Provisional data.
2. Including middle schools deemed primary.
3. Including middle schools deemed secondary. Excluding sixth form colleges from 1995 onwards.
4. Teachers whose full-time service was divided between primary and secondary schools.

TEACHERS IN SERVICE
Graduate teachers in full-time service: degree subject by sex, sector and class of degree, 31 March 1999

ENGLAND AND WALES

	Degree subject group					
	Education	Medicine	Technology	Agriculture	Mathematics [1]	Other science
Men						
Maintained nursery, primary and secondary						
1st class honours	310	10	100	10	360	670
2nd class honours	10,640	160	1,800	270	2,990	10,390
Other degrees	8,490	70	1,560	80	2,820	6,460
Total	19,440	230	3,460	350	6,170	17,520
Special						
1st class honours	20	-	-	-	-	10
2nd class honours	500	-	30	10	40	190
Other degrees	470	-	30	-	50	180
Total	990	10	60	20	90	370
Other sectors[2]						
1st class honours	110	10	240	10	390	560
2nd class honours	1,800	110	1,230	200	1,400	4,070
Other degrees	1,400	80	1,010	70	1,040	2,130
Total	3,310	210	2,470	290	2,830	6,750
Total						
1st class honours	440	20	340	20	750	1,240
2nd class honours	12,940	270	3,050	480	4,430	14,640
Other degrees	10,360	150	2,590	150	3,910	8,770
Total	23,740	440	5,980	650	9,090	24,640
Women						
Maintained nursery, primary and secondary						
1st class honours	780	20	50	20	570	820
2nd class honours	21,810	490	590	370	5,220	12,930
Other degrees	15,030	130	310	60	2,140	3,410
Total	37,620	640	950	450	7,930	17,160
Special						
1st class honours	30	-	-	-	-	10
2nd class honours	970	20	10	10	70	250
Other degrees	960	10	10	-	40	100
Total	1,960	30	20	10	110	360
Other sectors[2]						
1st class honours	140	40	20	10	210	260
2nd class honours	2,400	230	140	80	950	2,420
Other degrees	1,730	170	80	40	590	760
Total	4,270	430	240	120	1,750	3,440
Total						
1st class honours	960	60	70	20	780	1,080
2nd class honours	25,170	740	750	450	6,240	15,600
Other degrees	17,720	310	400	110	2,770	4,280
Total	43,850	1,110	1,210	580	9,790	20,960
Men and Women						
Maintained nursery, primary and secondary	57,060	870	4,410	790	14,100	34,680
Special	2,950	40	80	30	200	730
Other sectors[2]	7,580	640	2,710	410	4,580	10,190
Total	67,590	1,550	7,200	1,230	18,880	45,590

24a TEACHERS IN SERVICE
Graduate teachers in full-time service: degree subject by sex, sector and class of degree, 31 March 1999

ENGLAND AND WALES

	Degree subject group					Total
	Social studies	Language studies	Arts other than languages	Music, drama and visual arts	Others	All subjects
Men						
Maintained nursery, primary and secondary						
1st class honours	210	400	260	280	20	2,620
2nd class honours	10,590	8,050	7,700	3,740	620	56,920
Other degrees	2,330	1,580	4,700	930	520	29,540
Total	13,130	10,030	12,660	4,950	1,160	89,080
Special						
1st class honours	10	10	-	-	-	50
2nd class honours	300	140	170	120	20	1,520
Other degrees	100	50	190	40	20	1,140
Total	410	200	360	170	40	2,700
Other sectors[2]						
1st class honours	380	380	240	210	30	2,550
2nd class honours	5,920	3,290	2,420	1,370	270	22,060
Other degrees	1,780	650	950	390	240	9,740
Total	8,070	4,320	3,610	1,970	540	34,360
Total						
1st class honours	590	780	500	500	50	5,220
2nd class honours	16,800	11,480	10,280	5,230	900	80,500
Other degrees	4,210	2,280	5,850	1,370	780	40,420
Total	21,610	14,540	16,630	7,090	1,740	126,140
Women						
Maintained nursery, primary and secondary						
1st class honours	520	1,000	430	490	70	4,760
2nd class honours	20,530	30,310	17,020	12,030	1,480	122,780
Other degrees	3,000	5,130	4,520	1,810	960	36,510
Total	24,050	36,440	21,970	14,320	2,510	164,040
Special						
1st class honours	10	10	10	10	-	90
2nd class honours	530	490	290	270	20	2,930
Other degrees	110	120	180	60	30	1,620
Total	650	610	480	350	60	4,640
Other sectors[2]						
1st class honours	310	370	120	160	20	1,660
2nd class honours	4,140	4,850	1,960	1,270	230	18,650
Other degrees	1,140	1,120	740	290	240	6,900
Total	5,580	6,340	2,830	1,710	500	27,210
Total						
1st class honours	850	1,380	550	650	100	6,500
2nd class honours	25,200	35,650	19,270	13,570	1,730	144,360
Other degrees	4,250	6,370	5,450	2,160	1,240	45,030
Total	30,290	43,390	25,270	16,380	3,060	195,900
Men and Women						
Maintained nursery, primary and secondary	37,180	46,470	34,630	19,270	3,680	253,130
Special	1,060	810	840	520	90	7,340
Other sectors[2]	13,650	10,650	6,440	3,680	1,030	61,570
Total	51,890	57,930	41,900	23,470	4,800	322,040

Source: Database of Teacher Records.

1. Mathematics includes statistics and computer studies.
2. Including independent schools, further and higher education and teachers whose service is divided between different types of establishment.

TEACHERS IN SERVICE

Graduate teachers in full-time service: degree subject by sex, sector and class of degree, 31 March 1999 [1]

ENGLAND ONLY

	Degree subject group					
	Education	Medicine	Technology	Agriculture	Mathematics [2]	Other science
Men						
Maintained nursery, primary and secondary						
1st class honours	290	10	100	10	340	620
2nd class honours	9,810	150	1,670	240	2,770	9,640
Other degrees	8,010	60	1,450	70	2,580	6,030
Total	18,120	220	3,220	320	5,700	16,300
Special						
1st class honours	10	-	-	-	-	10
2nd class honours	450	-	30	10	40	180
Other degrees	450	-	30	-	50	170
Total	920	10	60	20	90	360
Other sectors[3]						
1st class honours	100	10	210	10	380	530
2nd class honours	1,710	110	1,150	180	1,330	3,880
Other degrees	1,340	80	940	70	1,000	2,050
Total	3,160	200	2,300	260	2,700	6,460
Total						
1st class honours	410	20	320	20	720	1,160
2nd class honours	11,980	260	2,840	440	4,140	13,700
Other degrees	9,810	150	2,420	140	3,630	8,250
Total	22,200	430	5,570	600	8,480	23,110
Women						
Maintained nursery, primary and secondary						
1st class honours	720	20	50	10	530	770
2nd class honours	20,370	480	570	350	4,890	12,210
Other degrees	14,260	130	300	60	2,000	3,230
Total	35,350	620	910	420	7,410	16,200
Special						
1st class honours	30	-	-	-	-	10
2nd class honours	910	20	10	10	70	240
Other degrees	940	10	10	-	40	100
Total	1,880	30	20	10	110	340
Other sectors[3]						
1st class honours	130	40	20	10	200	250
2nd class honours	2,280	230	140	70	920	2,330
Other degrees	1,660	160	70	40	570	730
Total	4,080	430	230	120	1,680	3,310
Total						
1st class honours	880	60	70	20	730	1,020
2nd class honours	23,570	720	720	430	5,870	14,770
Other degrees	16,860	300	380	110	2,610	4,050
Total	41,310	1,080	1,170	560	9,200	19,850
Men and Women						
Maintained nursery, primary and secondary	53,470	840	4,140	750	13,110	32,500
Special	2,800	40	80	30	200	700
Other sectors[3]	7,230	630	2,530	380	4,380	9,760
Total	63,500	1,500	6,740	1,150	17,680	42,960

TEACHERS IN SERVICE

24b

Graduate teachers in full-time service: degree subject by sex, sector and class of degree, 31 March 1999 [1]

ENGLAND ONLY

	Degree subject group					Total
	Social studies	Language studies	Arts other than languages	Music, drama and visual arts	Others	All subjects
Men						
Maintained nursery, primary and secondary						
1st class honours	200	370	240	260	20	2,460
2nd class honours	9,940	7,550	7,180	3,470	580	53,010
Other degrees	2,180	1,470	4,430	870	480	27,650
Total	12,330	9,390	11,850	4,600	1,080	83,110
Special						
1st class honours	10	10	-	-	-	50
2nd class honours	290	140	160	120	10	1,440
Other degrees	100	50	190	40	20	1,100
Total	400	200	350	170	40	2,590
Other sectors[3]						
1st class honours	370	370	240	200	30	2,430
2nd class honours	5,650	3,170	2,340	1,300	250	21,070
Other degrees	1,710	630	910	370	230	9,320
Total	7,720	4,160	3,480	1,870	520	32,820
Total						
1st class honours	570	750	480	460	50	4,940
2nd class honours	15,880	10,860	9,670	4,890	850	75,520
Other degrees	3,990	2,140	5,520	1,280	740	38,070
Total	20,440	13,740	15,680	6,630	1,640	118,520
Women						
Maintained nursery, primary and secondary						
1st class honours	490	930	390	470	70	4,450
2nd class honours	19,300	27,990	15,810	11,200	1,420	114,570
Other degrees	2,830	4,780	4,280	1,690	930	34,490
Total	22,630	33,690	20,490	13,360	2,420	153,500
Special						
1st class honours	10	10	10	10	-	80
2nd class honours	510	470	280	250	20	2,800
Other degrees	100	110	180	60	30	1,580
Total	630	590	460	320	60	4,460
Other sectors[3]						
1st class honours	290	360	110	150	20	1,580
2nd class honours	3,950	4,680	1,900	1,220	220	17,930
Other degrees	1,090	1,080	710	280	230	6,620
Total	5,330	6,130	2,720	1,650	470	26,120
Total						
1st class honours	800	1,300	510	630	90	6,110
2nd class honours	23,760	33,140	17,990	12,680	1,660	135,290
Other degrees	4,030	5,970	5,170	2,030	1,190	42,690
Total	28,590	40,410	23,670	15,330	2,940	184,090
Men and Women						
Maintained nursery, primary and secondary	34,960	43,080	32,330	17,960	3,500	236,610
Special	1,030	790	810	490	90	7,050
Other sectors[3]	13,050	10,290	6,200	3,520	980	58,940
Total	49,030	54,150	39,340	21,960	4,570	302,600

Source: Database of Teacher Records.

1. Provisional data.
2. Mathematics includes statistics and computer studies.
3. Including independent schools, further and higher education and teachers whose service is divided between different types of establishment.

TEACHERS IN SERVICE
Full-time teachers at March 1999[1]: grade and sex by sector and length of experience

25a

ENGLAND AND WALES

(thousands)

	Teachers in each length of service band								
	Head			Deputy Head			Classroom		
	Men	Women	Total	Men	Women	Total	Men	Women	Total
Nursery and primary									
0 - 4 years	-	-	-	0.1	0.1	0.2	6.3	41.8	48.1
5 - 9 years	0.1	0.3	0.4	0.5	1.4	2.0	3.5	24.2	27.6
10 - 14 years	0.5	1.1	1.6	0.7	2.2	2.9	1.5	16.5	18.0
15 - 19 years	0.8	2.4	3.2	0.5	2.8	3.3	1.1	18.3	19.4
20 + years	7.0	8.0	15.0	2.6	5.2	7.8	4.8	26.5	31.2
Total	8.4	11.8	20.2	4.4	11.7	16.1	17.1	127.2	144.3
Secondary									
0 - 4 years	-	-	-	-	-	-	17.4	26.5	43.9
5 - 9 years	-	-	-	-	-	0.1	11.0	15.0	26.0
10 - 14 years	-	-	0.1	0.3	0.2	0.5	8.1	13.1	21.2
15 - 19 years	0.3	0.2	0.5	0.6	0.6	1.2	10.7	17.6	28.3
20 + years	2.8	0.9	3.7	3.5	1.6	5.1	33.1	24.8	58.0
Total	3.1	1.2	4.3	4.4	2.5	6.9	80.3	97.0	177.3
Special									
0 - 4 years	-	-	-	-	-	-	0.5	1.2	1.7
5 - 9 years	-	-	-	-	-	0.1	0.4	1.3	1.7
10 - 14 years	-	-	0.1	-	0.1	0.2	0.4	1.6	2.0
15 - 19 years	0.1	0.1	0.2	0.1	0.2	0.3	0.6	1.9	2.6
20 + years	0.5	0.3	0.9	0.3	0.3	0.7	1.3	2.4	3.7
Total	0.7	0.5	1.2	0.5	0.7	1.2	3.4	8.3	11.7
All sectors									
0 - 4 years	-	-	-	0.1	0.1	0.2	24.2	69.4	93.6
5 - 9 years	0.1	0.3	0.4	0.6	1.5	2.1	14.9	40.4	55.3
10 - 14 years	0.6	1.2	1.7	1.0	2.6	3.5	10.0	31.2	41.2
15 - 19 years	1.2	2.7	3.9	1.2	3.6	4.8	12.4	37.8	50.2
20 + years	10.3	9.3	19.6	6.4	7.1	13.5	39.2	53.7	92.9
Total	12.2	13.5	25.7	9.3	14.8	24.1	100.8	232.5	333.2

TEACHERS IN SERVICE
Full-time teachers at March 1999[1]: grade and sex by sector and length of experience

ENGLAND AND WALES   (thousands)

| | Teachers in each length of service band | | | | | |
| | Other [2] | | | Total | | |
	Men	Women	Total	Men	Women	Total
Nursery and primary						
0 - 4 years	-	0.1	0.2	6.4	42.5	48.9
5 - 9 years	-	-	-	4.1	25.9	30.0
10 - 14 years	-	-	-	2.6	19.8	22.5
15 - 19 years	-	-	-	2.4	23.5	25.8
20 + years	-	-	-	14.4	39.7	54.0
Total	-	0.2	0.2	29.9	151.3	181.3
Secondary						
0 - 4 years	0.1	0.1	0.2	17.7	27.0	44.6
5 - 9 years	-	-	-	11.1	15.0	26.1
10 - 14 years	-	-	-	8.4	13.4	21.8
15 - 19 years	-	-	-	11.6	18.4	30.0
20 + years	-	-	-	39.4	27.3	66.7
Total	0.1	0.2	0.3	88.1	101.1	189.3
Special						
0 - 4 years	-	-	-	0.6	1.2	1.7
5 - 9 years	-	-	-	0.5	1.3	1.8
10 - 14 years	-	-	-	0.5	1.7	2.2
15 - 19 years	-	-	-	0.9	2.2	3.1
20 + years	-	-	-	2.2	3.1	5.3
Total	-	-	-	4.6	9.5	14.1
All sectors						
0 - 4 years	0.1	0.3	0.4	24.7	70.7	95.3
5 - 9 years	-	-	0.1	15.7	42.2	57.9
10 - 14 years	-	-	-	11.6	34.9	46.5
15 - 19 years	-	-	-	14.8	44.1	58.9
20 + years	-	-	-	56.0	70.1	126.0
Total	0.1	0.3	0.5	122.7	262.0	384.6

Source: Database of Teacher Records.

1. Provisional 1999 estimates.
2. Mainly teachers without qualified teacher status.

TEACHERS IN SERVICE
Full-time teachers at March 1999: grade and sex by sector and length of experience

ENGLAND ONLY
(thousands)

| | Teachers in each length of service band | | | | | | | | |
| | Head | | | Deputy Head | | | Classroom | | |
	Men	Women	Total	Men	Women	Total	Men	Women	Total
Nursery and primary									
0 - 4 years	-	-	-	-	0.1	0.1	5.9	39.6	45.4
5 - 9 years	0.1	0.3	0.4	0.5	1.3	1.8	3.2	22.6	25.9
10 - 14 years	0.4	1.0	1.4	0.6	2.1	2.7	1.4	15.4	16.8
15 - 19 years	0.7	2.2	2.9	0.4	2.6	3.1	1.0	17.1	18.1
20 + years	6.4	7.4	13.7	2.4	4.7	7.1	4.5	24.4	28.9
Total	7.6	10.9	18.5	4.0	10.8	14.8	16.0	119.1	135.1
Secondary									
0 - 4 years	-	-	-	-	-	-	16.4	25.0	41.4
5 - 9 years	-	-	-	-	-	0.1	10.4	14.0	24.3
10 - 14 years	-	-	0.1	0.2	0.2	0.5	7.6	12.2	19.8
15 - 19 years	0.3	0.2	0.5	0.6	0.6	1.2	10.0	16.4	26.4
20 + years	2.6	0.9	3.5	3.2	1.5	4.7	30.9	23.0	53.9
Total	2.9	1.2	4.0	4.1	2.3	6.4	75.3	90.6	165.8
Special									
0 - 4 years	-	-	-	-	-	-	0.5	1.1	1.6
5 - 9 years	-	-	-	-	-	0.1	0.4	1.2	1.6
10 - 14 years	-	-	0.1	-	0.1	0.2	0.4	1.5	1.9
15 - 19 years	0.1	0.1	0.2	0.1	0.2	0.3	0.6	1.9	2.5
20 + years	0.5	0.3	0.8	0.3	0.3	0.6	1.3	2.3	3.6
Total	0.6	0.5	1.1	0.5	0.6	1.1	3.2	8.0	11.2
All sectors									
0 - 4 years	-	-	-	0.1	0.1	0.2	22.8	65.7	88.5
5 - 9 years	0.1	0.3	0.4	0.5	1.4	2.0	14.0	37.8	51.8
10 - 14 years	0.5	1.1	1.6	0.9	2.4	3.3	9.4	29.1	38.5
15 - 19 years	1.1	2.5	3.6	1.2	3.3	4.5	11.6	35.3	47.0
20 + years	9.4	8.6	18.0	6.0	6.5	12.5	36.6	49.8	86.4
Total	11.1	12.6	23.7	8.6	13.8	22.4	94.5	217.7	312.2

25b

TEACHERS IN SERVICE

Full-time teachers at March 1999: grade and sex by sector and length of experience

ENGLAND ONLY

(thousands)

| | Teachers in each length of service band | | | | | |
| | Other [1] | | | Total | | |
	Men	Women	Total	Men	Women	Total
Nursery and primary						
0 - 4 years	-	0.1	0.2	6.0	40.2	46.2
5 - 9 years	-	-	-	3.8	24.3	28.1
10 - 14 years	-	-	-	2.4	18.5	20.9
15 - 19 years	-	-	-	2.2	21.9	24.1
20 + years	-	-	-	13.3	36.5	49.8
Total	-	0.2	0.2	27.7	141.4	169.1
Secondary						
0 - 4 years	0.1	0.1	0.2	16.7	25.4	42.1
5 - 9 years	-	-	-	10.4	14.1	24.5
10 - 14 years	-	-	-	7.9	12.4	20.3
15 - 19 years	-	-	-	10.8	17.2	28.0
20 + years	-	-	-	36.7	25.4	62.1
Total	0.1	0.2	0.3	82.5	94.5	177.1
Special						
0 - 4 years	-	-	-	0.5	1.1	1.7
5 - 9 years	-	-	-	0.4	1.2	1.7
10 - 14 years	-	-	-	0.5	1.7	2.2
15 - 19 years	-	-	-	0.8	2.2	3.0
20 + years	-	-	-	2.1	3.0	5.0
Total	-	-	-	4.4	9.2	13.5
All sectors						
0 - 4 years	0.1	0.3	0.4	23.2	66.8	90.0
5 - 9 years	-	-	0.1	14.7	39.6	54.3
10 - 14 years	-	-	-	10.8	32.6	43.4
15 - 19 years	-	-	-	13.9	41.2	55.1
20 + years	-	-	-	52.1	64.9	117.0
Total	0.1	0.3	0.5	114.6	245.1	359.7

Source: Database of Teacher Records.

1. Mainly teachers without qualified teacher status.

26a TEACHERS IN SERVICE
Full-time teachers in maintained nursery, primary, secondary and special schools by sector, grade age and sex, March 1999

ENGLAND AND WALES (thousands)

	Nursery and Primary					Secondary				
	Heads	Deputy heads	Classroom	Other [1]	total	Heads	Deputy heads	Classroom	Other [1]	total
Men										
Under 25	-	-	0.9	-	0.9	-	-	2.0	0.1	2.0
25-29	-	0.1	3.3	-	3.4	-	-	9.3	0.1	9.4
30-34	0.1	0.5	2.9	-	3.6	-	-	9.3	0.1	9.4
35-39	0.5	0.6	2.2	-	3.2	0.1	0.3	9.6	-	10.0
40-44	1.3	0.8	2.2	-	4.3	0.3	0.8	13.1	-	14.2
45-49	2.8	1.3	3.1	-	7.1	1.0	1.4	19.2	-	21.6
50-54	2.7	0.9	2.0	-	5.6	1.1	1.3	13.4	-	15.9
55-59	0.9	0.2	0.5	-	1.6	0.5	0.5	3.7	-	4.7
60-64	0.1	-	0.1	-	0.2	0.1	0.1	0.7	-	0.9
65 and over	-	-	-	-	-	-	-	-	-	-
All ages	8.4	4.4	17.1	0.1	29.9	3.1	4.4	80.3	0.3	88.1
Women										
Under 25	-	-	9.3	0.2	9.5	-	-	4.5	0.1	4.6
25-29	-	0.2	24.4	0.2	24.7	-	-	16.6	0.2	16.8
30-34	0.2	1.3	15.6	0.1	17.2	-	-	11.8	0.1	11.9
35-39	0.6	1.3	10.5	0.1	12.5	-	0.2	10.4	0.1	10.7
40-44	1.8	2.3	17.5	-	21.7	0.2	0.6	15.6	-	16.4
45-49	3.8	3.5	25.6	-	33.0	0.4	0.8	19.6	-	20.8
50-54	3.6	2.3	17.8	-	23.7	0.4	0.6	13.2	-	14.2
55-59	1.5	0.8	5.8	-	8.0	0.1	0.2	4.5	-	4.9
60-64	0.2	0.1	0.8	-	1.1	-	-	0.7	-	0.8
65 and over	-	-	-	-	0.1	-	-	-	-	-
All ages	11.8	11.7	127.2	0.6	151.3	1.2	2.5	97.0	0.5	101.1
Men and Women										
Under 25	-	-	10.2	0.2	10.4	-	-	6.5	0.2	6.7
25-29	-	0.2	27.6	0.2	28.1	-	-	25.9	0.3	26.2
30-34	0.4	1.8	18.5	0.1	20.7	-	0.1	21.1	0.1	21.3
35-39	1.0	1.9	12.7	0.1	15.7	0.1	0.6	20.0	0.1	20.8
40-44	3.1	3.1	19.7	-	26.0	0.5	1.3	28.7	0.1	30.6
45-49	6.6	4.8	28.7	-	40.1	1.4	2.2	38.8	-	42.4
50-54	6.3	3.2	19.7	-	29.3	1.5	1.9	26.6	-	30.1
55-59	2.4	1.0	6.2	-	9.6	0.6	0.7	8.3	-	9.6
60-64	0.3	0.1	0.9	-	1.3	0.1	0.1	1.5	-	1.7
65 and over	-	-	-	-	0.1	-	-	0.1	-	0.1
All ages	20.2	16.1	144.3	0.7	181.3	4.3	6.9	177.3	0.8	189.3

CONTINUED

TEACHERS IN SERVICE

Full-time teachers in maintained nursery, primary, secondary and special schools by sector, grade age and sex, March 1999

ENGLAND AND WALES

(thousands)

	Special					Total				
	Heads	Deputy heads	Classroom	Other [1]	total	Heads	Deputy heads	Classroom	Other [1]	total
Men										
Under 25	-	-	-	-	-	-	-	2.9	0.1	3.0
25-29	-	-	0.2	-	0.2	-	0.1	12.8	0.1	13.0
30-34	-	-	0.3	-	0.3	0.1	0.6	12.5	0.1	13.3
35-39	-	-	0.4	-	0.5	0.5	0.9	12.2	-	13.8
40-44	0.1	0.1	0.8	-	1.0	1.8	1.7	16.0	-	19.5
45-49	0.2	0.2	1.0	-	1.4	4.0	2.9	23.2	-	30.1
50-54	0.2	0.1	0.6	-	0.9	4.1	2.3	15.9	-	22.4
55-59	0.1	-	0.1	-	0.2	1.4	0.7	4.3	-	6.5
60-64	-	-	-	-	-	0.2	0.1	0.8	-	1.1
65 and over	-	-	-	-	-	-	-	-	-	0.1
All ages	0.7	0.5	3.4	-	4.6	12.2	9.3	100.8	0.4	122.7
Women										
Under 25	-	-	0.1	-	0.1	-	-	13.8	0.4	14.2
25-29	-	-	0.6	-	0.6	-	0.2	41.5	0.4	42.0
30-34	-	-	0.7	-	0.7	0.3	1.3	28.1	0.1	29.8
35-39	-	0.1	0.8	-	0.9	0.7	1.6	21.8	0.1	24.2
40-44	0.1	0.2	1.7	-	1.9	2.1	3.0	34.8	0.1	40.0
45-49	0.1	0.2	2.2	-	2.5	4.4	4.4	47.4	0.1	56.3
50-54	0.1	0.2	1.6	-	1.9	4.1	3.1	32.6	-	39.8
55-59	0.1	-	0.6	-	0.7	1.7	1.0	10.8	-	13.5
60-64	-	-	0.1	-	0.1	0.3	0.1	1.6	-	2.0
65 and over	-	-	-	-	-	-	-	0.1	-	0.1
All ages	0.5	0.7	8.3	-	9.5	13.5	14.8	232.5	1.1	262.0
Men and Women										
Under 25	-	-	0.1	-	0.1	-	-	16.7	0.5	17.2
25-29	-	-	0.8	-	0.8	-	0.2	54.3	0.5	55.0
30-34	-	-	1.0	-	1.0	0.4	1.9	40.6	0.2	43.1
35-39	0.1	0.1	1.3	-	1.4	1.2	2.6	34.0	0.2	37.9
40-44	0.2	0.3	2.4	-	2.9	3.9	4.7	50.8	0.1	59.5
45-49	0.4	0.4	3.2	-	3.9	8.4	7.3	70.6	0.1	86.4
50-54	0.4	0.3	2.2	-	2.8	8.2	5.4	48.5	-	62.1
55-59	0.1	0.1	0.7	-	0.9	3.1	1.7	15.2	-	20.0
60-64	-	-	0.1	-	0.1	0.5	0.2	2.4	-	3.1
65 and over	-	-	-	-	-	-	-	0.1	-	0.1
All ages	1.2	1.2	11.7	-	14.1	25.7	24.1	333.2	1.5	384.6

Source: Database of Teacher Records.

1. Mainly teachers without qualified teacher status.

TEACHERS IN SERVICE

Full-time teachers in maintained nursery, primary, secondary and special schools by sector, grade age and sex, March 1999

26b

ENGLAND ONLY (thousands)

	Nursery and Primary					Secondary				
	Heads	Deputy heads	Classroom	Other [1]	total	Heads	Deputy heads	Classroom	Other [1]	total
Men										
Under 25	-	-	0.8	-	0.9	-	-	1.8	0.1	1.9
25-29	-	0.1	3.0	-	3.1	-	-	8.8	0.1	8.8
30-34	0.1	0.4	2.7	-	3.3	-	-	8.8	-	8.9
35-39	0.4	0.5	2.1	-	3.0	0.1	0.3	9.0	-	9.4
40-44	1.2	0.7	2.0	-	3.9	0.3	0.7	12.3	-	13.3
45-49	2.5	1.2	2.9	-	6.6	0.9	1.3	18.0	-	20.2
50-54	2.5	0.8	1.9	-	5.2	1.1	1.2	12.5	-	14.9
55-59	0.8	0.2	0.5	-	1.5	0.4	0.4	3.4	-	4.3
60-64	0.1	-	0.1	-	0.2	0.1	-	0.7	-	0.8
65 and over	-	-	-	-	-	-	-	-	-	-
All ages	7.6	4.0	16.0	0.1	27.7	2.9	4.1	75.3	0.3	82.5
Women										
Under 25	-	-	8.8	0.2	9.0	-	-	4.2	0.1	4.3
25-29	-	0.2	22.9	0.2	23.2	-	-	15.6	0.2	15.7
30-34	0.2	1.2	14.6	0.1	16.1	-	-	11.1	0.1	11.2
35-39	0.5	1.2	9.8	0.1	11.6	-	0.2	9.7	-	10.0
40-44	1.7	2.1	16.3	-	20.1	0.2	0.6	14.5	-	15.3
45-49	3.6	3.2	24.0	-	30.8	0.4	0.7	18.3	-	19.4
50-54	3.3	2.1	16.6	-	22.1	0.3	0.5	12.3	-	13.2
55-59	1.4	0.7	5.4	-	7.5	0.1	0.2	4.2	-	4.6
60-64	0.2	0.1	0.7	-	1.0	-	-	0.7	-	0.8
65 and over	-	-	-	-	0.1	-	-	-	-	-
All ages	10.9	10.8	119.1	0.6	141.4	1.2	2.3	90.6	0.5	94.5
Men and Women										
Under 25	-	-	9.6	0.2	9.8	-	-	6.0	0.2	6.2
25-29	-	0.2	25.9	0.2	26.3	-	-	24.3	0.3	24.6
30-34	0.3	1.7	17.3	0.1	19.4	-	0.1	19.8	0.1	20.0
35-39	1.0	1.8	11.9	0.1	14.6	0.1	0.5	18.7	0.1	19.4
40-44	2.8	2.8	18.3	-	24.0	0.5	1.3	26.8	0.1	28.6
45-49	6.1	4.4	26.9	-	37.4	1.3	2.0	36.2	-	39.7
50-54	5.8	3.0	18.5	-	27.2	1.4	1.8	24.8	-	28.1
55-59	2.2	0.9	5.9	-	9.0	0.6	0.6	7.7	-	8.9
60-64	0.3	0.1	0.8	-	1.2	0.1	0.1	1.4	-	1.5
65 and over	-	-	-	-	0.1	-	-	0.1	-	0.1
All ages	18.5	14.8	135.1	0.6	169.1	4.0	6.4	165.8	0.7	177.1

CONTINUED
TEACHERS IN SERVICE
Full-time teachers in maintained nursery, primary, secondary and special schools by sector, grade age and sex, March 1999

ENGLAND ONLY   (thousands)

	Special					Total				
	Heads	Deputy heads	Classroom	Other [1]	total	Heads	Deputy heads	Classroom	Other [1]	total
Men										
Under 25	-	-	-	-	-	-	-	2.7	0.1	2.8
25-29	-	-	0.2	-	0.2	-	0.1	11.9	0.1	12.1
30-34	-	-	0.2	-	0.3	0.1	0.5	11.7	0.1	12.4
35-39	-	-	0.4	-	0.5	0.5	0.9	11.5	-	12.9
40-44	0.1	0.1	0.7	-	1.0	1.6	1.6	15.0	-	18.2
45-49	0.2	0.2	0.9	-	1.3	3.6	2.7	21.8	-	28.2
50-54	0.2	0.1	0.6	-	0.9	3.8	2.2	14.9	-	20.9
55-59	0.1	-	0.1	-	0.2	1.3	0.6	4.0	-	6.0
60-64	-	-	-	-	-	0.2	0.1	0.8	-	1.0
65 and over	-	-	-	-	-	-	-	-	-	0.1
All ages	0.6	0.5	3.2	-	4.4	11.1	8.6	94.5	0.4	114.6
Women										
Under 25	-	-	0.1	-	0.1	-	-	13.0	0.3	13.4
25-29	-	-	0.5	-	0.5	-	0.2	39.0	0.3	39.5
30-34	-	-	0.7	-	0.7	0.2	1.3	26.4	0.1	28.0
35-39	-	0.1	0.8	-	0.9	0.6	1.5	20.3	0.1	22.6
40-44	0.1	0.1	1.6	-	1.9	2.0	2.8	32.4	0.1	37.3
45-49	0.1	0.2	2.1	-	2.5	4.1	4.1	44.4	0.1	52.7
50-54	0.1	0.1	1.5	-	1.8	3.8	2.8	30.5	-	37.1
55-59	0.1	-	0.5	-	0.7	1.6	1.0	10.2	-	12.7
60-64	-	-	0.1	-	0.1	0.3	0.1	1.5	-	1.9
65 and over	-	-	-	-	-	-	-	0.1	-	0.1
All ages	0.5	0.6	8.0	-	9.2	12.6	13.8	217.7	1.1	245.1
Men and Women										
Under 25	-	-	0.1	-	0.1	-	-	15.7	0.4	16.2
25-29	-	-	0.7	-	0.7	-	0.2	50.9	0.5	51.6
30-34	-	-	0.9	-	1.0	0.3	1.8	38.1	0.2	40.4
35-39	0.1	0.1	1.2	-	1.4	1.1	2.4	31.8	0.2	35.5
40-44	0.2	0.3	2.3	-	2.8	3.6	4.4	47.4	0.1	55.5
45-49	0.4	0.4	3.1	-	3.8	7.8	6.8	66.2	0.1	80.8
50-54	0.3	0.3	2.1	-	2.7	7.6	5.0	45.4	-	58.0
55-59	0.1	0.1	0.7	-	0.9	2.9	1.6	14.2	-	18.7
60-64	-	-	0.1	-	0.1	0.5	0.2	2.3	-	2.9
65 and over	-	-	-	-	-	-	-	0.1	-	0.1
All ages	1.1	1.1	11.2	-	13.5	23.7	22.4	312.2	1.4	359.7

Source: Database of Teacher Records.

1. Mainly unqualified teachers.

TEACHERS IN SERVICE
Full-time teachers in maintained secondary schools: age at November 1996 by subject of qualification [1]

ENGLAND

	Percentages					Total numbers (000s)
	Under 30	30-39	40-49	50 or over	Total	
Subject:						
Mathematics	15	22	43	20	100	27.1
English	16	23	44	17	100	31.6
Biology	16	24	44	15	100	11.3
Chemistry	14	20	42	23	100	10.7
Physics	11	21	44	24	100	10.4
General Science	20	25	39	16	100	15.5
Other Sciences	16	28	39	18	100	6.2
French	19	25	41	15	100	15.5
German	23	24	40	13	100	6.9
Spanish	28	26	34	12	100	2.5
Other Modern Languages	25	23	38	14	100	2.7
Design & Technology	13	25	43	19	100	11.1
Information Technology	18	23	47	12	100	4.9
Other Technology	18	27	37	18	100	4.4
Home Economics	7	22	49	22	100	6.8
Business Studies	24	26	34	16	100	4.3
Classics	9	22	32	38	100	1.4
History	16	23	43	18	100	19.2
Religious Education	17	24	40	20	100	8.6
Geography	16	21	49	14	100	15.6
Other Social Studies	14	23	48	15	100	11.3
Combined Arts/Humanities/ Social Studies	15	23	43	19	100	4.2
Music	23	24	36	16	100	6.3
Drama	20	29	41	10	100	8.0
Art	12	23	45	20	100	10.8
Physical Education	19	27	43	11	100	22.0
Careers	3	12	55	30	100	0.9
Personal and Social Education	15	21	49	15	100	2.3
General Studies	12	23	46	20	100	2.2
General Primary Subjects	8	22	62	8	100	1.0
Other	10	21	48	21	100	21.5
Total [1]	16	24	43	17	100	307.2
Full-time teachers	17	24	43	17	100	170.1

Source: 1996/97 Secondary Schools Curriculum and Staffing Survey

1. Teachers are counted once against each subject in which they have a post A level qualification.

TEACHERS IN SERVICE

Full-time teachers in maintained secondary schools – highest level of qualification [1] by subject of qualification [2], at November 1996

ENGLAND

Subject:	Percentages						Total numbers (000s)
	Degree [3]	BEd	PGCE	Cert Ed	Other qual.	Total	
Mathematics	47	18	15	17	3	100	27.1
English	49	18	14	18	1	100	31.6
Biology	55	13	14	18	1	100	11.3
Chemistry	66	10	14	10	-	100	10.7
Physics	53	12	20	13	2	100	10.4
General Science	29	13	44	13	1	100	15.5
Other Sciences	66	10	12	10	2	100	6.2
French	59	12	16	10	2	100	15.5
German	64	11	18	4	3	100	6.9
Spanish	68	5	21	-	6	100	2.5
Other Modern Languages	68	5	18	4	5	100	2.7
Design & Technology	16	32	13	35	4	100	11.1
Information Technology	36	17	19	8	20	100	4.9
Other Technology	47	13	6	19	15	100	4.4
Home Economics	13	25	4	55	3	100	6.8
Business Studies	31	22	18	17	12	100	4.3
Classics	83	3	7	2	6	100	1.4
History	54	14	14	17	1	100	19.2
Religious Education	34	20	17	26	3	100	8.6
Geography	43	22	12	23	1	100	15.6
Other Social Studies	70	14	8	6	3	100	11.3
Combined Arts/Humanities/ Social Studies	55	19	14	11	1	100	4.2
Music	49	16	9	23	2	100	6.3
Drama	27	19	25	25	4	100	8.0
Art	42	17	9	30	3	100	10.8
Physical Education	13	37	11	38	1	100	22.0
Careers Education	11	10	11	20	48	100	0.9
Personal and Social Education	24	17	22	20	16	100	2.3
General Studies	20	23	28	24	5	100	2.2
General Primary Subjects	14	9	48	21	8	100	1.0
Other	45	13	10	10	22	100	21.5
Total [2]	44	18	15	19	4	100	307.2

Source: 1996/97 Secondary Schools Curriculum and Staffing Survey.

1. Where a teacher has more than one post A level qualification in the same subject, the qualification level is determined by the highest level reading from left (Degree) to right (Other Qualifications). For example, teachers shown under PGCE PGCE have a PGCE but not a degree or BEd in the subject, while those with a PGCE and a degree are shown only under Degree.

2. Teachers are counted once against each subject in which they have a post A level qualification.

3. Includes higher degrees but excludes BEds.

29 TEACHERS IN SERVICE

Full-time teachers in maintained secondary schools teaching named subjects : highest level of qualification[1] in subjects taught[2] to years 7-13, at November 1996

ENGLAND

Subject:	Degree [3]	BEd	PGCE	Cert Ed	Other qual.	No qual	Total	Total numbers (000s)
Mathematics	40	16	11	12	2	20	100	25.2
English	43	14	9	12	-	22	100	28.4
Biology [4]	63	11	15	5	-	6	100	5.1
Chemistry [4]	75	5	15	2	-	3	100	4.6
Physics [4]	62	8	21	3	-	6	100	4.4
General Science [4]	57	12	13	9	-	9	100	27.3
Other Sciences	23	-	4	2	-	71	100	1.6
French	50	10	13	7	2	18	100	16.2
German	47	8	14	2	2	27	100	8.1
Spanish	45	3	13	-	4	35	100	2.7
Other Modern Languages	22	2	3	-	1	73	100	1.3
Design & Technology [5]	13	18	6	20	1	42	100	18.6
Information Technology [5]	10	5	5	3	5	73	100	10.7
Combined Technology [5]	14	21	5	19	2	39	100	5.2
Home Economics	8	20	3	44	2	23	100	5.0
Business Studies	16	13	11	9	4	47	100	6.4
Classics	57	-	-	-	-	43	100	0.5
History	47	10	10	8	1	25	100	13.8
Religious Education	19	10	7	9	1	55	100	13.4
Geography	38	15	8	11	-	27	100	14.2
Other Social Studies	36	6	5	2	1	50	100	5.0
Combined Arts/Humanities/ Social Studies	8	3	2	1	-	85	100	6.3
Music	49	13	8	15	2	13	100	5.6
Drama	16	10	9	11	2	53	100	8.9
Art	41	12	7	18	2	19	100	9.4
Physical Education	11	34	5	23	-	26	100	20.0
Careers Education	2	1	1	3	3	91	100	1.9
Personal and Social Education	1	-	-	-	-	98	100	74.2
General Studies	1	2	2	1	-	94	100	7.9
Other	.	.	.	.	.	.	.	27.8
Total [2,6]	27	10	7	9	1	46	100	379.7

Source : 1996/97 Secondary Schools Curriculum and Staffing Survey.

1. Where a teacher has more than one post A level qualification in the same subject, the qualification level is determined by the highest level reading from left (Degree) to right (Other Qualifications). For example, teachers shown under PGCE have a PGCE but not a degree or BEd in the subject, while those with a PGCE and a degree are shown only under Degree.
2. Teachers are counted once against each subject which they are teaching.
3. Includes higher degrees but excludes BEds.
4. Teachers qualified in general science are treated as qualified to teach biology, chemistry, or physics. Teachers qualified in biology, chemistry or physics are treated as qualified to teach general science.
5. Teachers qualified in other technology are treated as qualified to teach design & technology or information technology. Teachers qualified in design and technology or information technology are treated as qualified to teach combined technology.
6. 'Other' not included in total percentages.

TEACHERS IN SERVICE

30 Full-time teachers in maintained secondary schools - Highest level of qualification [1] in subjects taught [2] to years 7-13 by percentage of periods taught in subject, at November 1996

ENGLAND

Subject:	Percentage of periods taught in subject							Tuition in subject as percentage of all tuition
	Degree [3]	BEd	PGCE	Cert Ed	Other qual.	No qual.	Total	
Mathematics	47	18	12	12	2	9	100	11.7
English	53	15	10	12	-	10	100	11.8
Biology [4]	67	9	13	5	-	5	100	1.0
Chemistry [4]	80	5	11	2	-	1	100	0.9
Physics [4]	67	7	20	3	-	3	100	0.8
Combined/General Science [4]	59	12	14	10	-	5	100	12.0
Other Sciences	28	-	5	3	-	64	100	0.3
French	55	11	13	8	2	10	100	6.1
German	55	9	15	3	1	17	100	2.3
Spanish	55	3	12	-	5	25	100	0.7
Other Modern Languages	29	2	3	-	3	63	100	0.3
Design and Technology [5]	14	22	7	24	1	31	100	7.4
Information Technology [5]	16	7	7	4	7	58	100	2.0
Combined Technology [5]	14	23	5	24	2	33	100	1.3
Home Economics	9	24	4	44	2	17	100	1.2
Business Studies	21	17	13	12	5	31	100	1.9
Classics	83	-	-	-	-	17	100	0.2
History	59	11	11	7	-	12	100	4.7
Religious Education	35	17	12	14	1	21	100	3.2
Geography	51	16	10	11	-	11	100	5.1
Other Social Studies	44	7	6	3	1	40	100	1.0
Combined Arts/Humanities/ Social Studies	9	4	2	2	-	82	100	1.3
Music	56	15	9	15	2	3	100	2.5
Drama	25	15	9	15	4	32	100	2.0
Art	50	13	8	20	2	7	100	4.1
Physical Education	15	47	5	27	-	6	100	7.1
Careers Education	1	2	1	6	3	87	100	0.1
Personal and Social Education	1	1	-	1	1	96	100	3.1
General Studies	3	9	6	1	-	81	100	0.4
Other	.	.	.	.	.	.	.	3.4
Total [2, 6]	42	16	10	13	1	18	100	100.0

Source : 1996/97 Secondary Schools Curriculum and Staffing Survey.

1. Where a teacher has more than one post A level qualification in the same subject, the qualification level is determined by the highest level reading from left (Degree) to right (Other Qualifications). For example, teachers shown under PGCE have a PGCE but not a degree on BEd in the subject, while those with a PGCE and a degree are shown only under Degree.
2. Teachers are counted once against each subject which they are teaching.
3. Includes higher degrees but excludes BEds.
4. Teachers qualified in general science are treated as qualified to teach biology, chemistry, or physics. Teachers qualified in biology, chemistry, or physics are treated as qualified to teach general science.
5. Teachers qualified in other technology are treated as qualified to teach design & technology or information technology.
   Teachers qualified in design and technology or information technology are treated as qualified to teach combined technology.
6. 'Other' not included in total percentages.

TEACHERS IN SERVICE
Advanced Skills Teachers in post in the maintained sector by Government Office region January 2000

ENGLAND

	Nursery and primary	Secondary	Special	Other	Total
Government Office region					
North East	-	20	-	0	30
North West	20	40	0	0	60
Yorkshire and The Humber	10	20	-	0	30
East Midlands	-	40	0	-	40
West Midlands	10	20	0	0	30
East of England	10	60	0	0	60
London	10	50	10	0	60
South East	30	40	-	0	70
South West	10	30	-	0	40
England	100	300	10	-	420

Source: DfEE annual 618G survey.

Teachers that had passed assessment to become an Advanced Skills Teacher at January 2000

	Nursery and primary	Secondary	Special	Other	Total
Government Office region					
North East	-	20	-	0	30
North West	20	60	0	0	70
Yorkshire and The Humber	10	30	-	0	50
East Midlands	10	50	0	0	60
West Midlands	10	30	0	0	40
East of England	20	80	-	0	90
London	10	60	10	0	70
South East	30	50	-	0	80
South West	10	40	-	0	50
England	120	400	20	0	540

Source: Westminster Education Consultants (WEC).

1. Data includes all candidates who passed their assessment before 20 January 2000

TEACHERS PAY
Full-time teachers in maintained nursery, primary, secondary and special schools – age distribution and spine point [1]: March 1999 [2]

ENGLAND AND WALES   i. Men

	Percentage of teachers in each age band							Total numbers (thousands)
	Classroom teachers' pay spine [1]				Deputy heads	Heads	Total	
	0 - 8.5	9	9.5 - 13.5	14 - 17				
Nursery & Primary								
Under 25	99.9	-	-	-	0.1	-	100	0.9
25-29	91.6	3.5	2.8	-	1.9	0.2	100	3.4
30-34	42.2	13.0	26.9	0.1	14.0	3.7	100	3.6
35-39	22.5	15.2	29.4	0.2	18.6	14.1	100	3.2
40-44	8.0	12.4	29.6	0.4	19.0	30.6	100	4.3
45-49	2.5	11.6	28.2	0.5	18.3	39.0	100	7.1
50-54	1.0	10.0	23.3	0.6	16.0	49.1	100	5.6
55-59	0.4	9.2	20.3	0.6	13.1	56.5	100	1.6
60 and over	-	17.5	26.5	0.9	8.5	46.6	100	0.2
All ages	22.7	10.6	23.3	0.4	14.7	28.3	100	29.9
Secondary								
Under 25	100.0	-	-	-	-	-	100	2.0
25-29	88.4	5.6	5.9	-	-	-	100	9.4
30-34	40.7	13.8	43.6	1.4	0.5	-	100	9.4
35-39	14.9	12.9	63.9	4.5	3.2	0.6	100	10.0
40-44	5.4	12.2	67.5	7.0	5.5	2.4	100	14.2
45-49	2.3	10.7	66.7	9.1	6.6	4.6	100	21.6
50-54	1.1	11.0	61.4	10.8	8.5	7.3	100	15.9
55-59	0.7	13.5	54.6	11.0	10.1	10.2	100	4.7
60 and over	1.0	22.6	53.0	7.6	6.1	9.7	100	0.9
All ages	19.4	11.1	54.4	6.6	5.1	3.5	100	88.1
Special								
Under 25	100.0	-	-	-	-	-	100	-
25-29	83.4	5.2	10.4	-	1.0	-	100	0.2
30-34	35.8	5.2	50.6	1.5	6.6	0.4	100	0.3
35-39	11.2	4.3	67.9	2.6	7.5	6.5	100	0.5
40-44	3.9	1.7	66.3	3.0	12.7	12.5	100	1.0
45-49	1.9	1.2	61.4	3.9	14.0	17.6	100	1.4
50-54	1.2	0.9	58.6	2.7	13.2	23.3	100	0.9
55-59	0.9	0.9	50.7	1.7	14.8	31.0	100	0.2
60 and over	2.2	2.2	55.6	6.7	8.9	24.4	100	-
All ages	9.2	2.0	58.8	2.9	11.8	15.3	100	4.6

Source: Database of Teacher Records.

1. Teachers not on a spine point are allocated to the nearest point according to their salary.
2. Provisional estimates.

32

Full-time teachers in maintained nursery, primary, secondary and special schools – age distribution and spine point [1]: March 1999 [2]

ENGLAND AND WALES   ii. Women

	Percentage of teachers in each age band							Total numbers (thousands)
	Classroom teachers' pay spine [1]				Deputy heads	Heads	Total	
	0 - 8.5	9	9.5 - 13.5	14 - 17				
Nursery & Primary								
Under 25	99.9	-	-	-	-	-	100	9.5
25-29	82.0	11.2	6.0	-	0.8	-	100	24.7
30-34	25.9	27.4	37.0	-	8.1	1.5	100	17.2
35-39	24.8	24.5	34.1	0.1	11.4	5.1	100	12.5
40-44	14.4	27.8	37.7	0.1	11.0	8.9	100	21.7
45-49	4.4	29.4	43.1	0.1	10.9	12.1	100	33.0
50-54	1.8	27.6	44.1	0.2	10.3	15.9	100	23.7
55-59	0.9	24.1	42.6	0.3	11.1	20.9	100	8.0
60 and over	0.5	18.3	37.5	0.1	10.9	32.7	100	1.1
All ages	27.7	23.2	32.4	0.1	8.3	8.3	100	151.3
Secondary								
Under 25	99.9	0.1	-	-	-	-	100	4.6
25-29	78.6	11.3	10.0	0.1	-	-	100	16.8
30-34	27.6	20.2	50.2	1.5	0.4	0.1	100	11.9
35-39	11.8	17.4	64.0	4.1	2.3	0.3	100	10.7
40-44	5.7	17.3	67.3	4.8	3.6	1.3	100	16.4
45-49	2.6	18.5	68.2	4.8	3.8	2.1	100	20.8
50-54	1.2	19.3	67.6	5.0	4.4	2.6	100	14.2
55-59	0.5	20.1	65.8	5.1	5.0	3.4	100	4.9
60 and over	0.2	20.4	60.9	5.4	7.5	5.6	100	0.8
All ages	23.4	16.6	52.8	3.4	2.6	1.3	100	101.1
Special								
Under 25	100.0	-	-	-	-	-	100	0.1
25-29	65.9	14.7	19.4	-	-	-	100	0.6
30-34	12.0	9.6	73.0	0.4	3.7	1.2	100	0.7
35-39	7.7	4.8	74.0	1.9	8.3	3.3	100	0.9
40-44	3.9	2.9	77.1	2.0	8.6	5.5	100	1.9
45-49	1.9	1.8	80.4	1.7	8.2	6.0	100	2.5
50-54	1.4	1.0	79.1	2.2	8.3	8.0	100	1.9
55-59	0.7	1.0	75.8	3.3	7.7	11.5	100	0.7
60 and over	-	4.8	63.5	1.6	6.3	23.8	100	0.1
All ages	8.2	3.5	73.5	1.8	7.4	5.7	100	9.5

Source: Database of Teacher Records.

1. Teachers not on a spine point are allocated to the nearest point according to their salary.
2. Provisional estimates.

CONTINUED
TEACHERS PAY
Full-time teachers in maintained nursery, primary, secondary and special schools – age distribution and spine point [1]: March 1999 [2]

ENGLAND AND WALES   ii. All teachers

	Percentage of teachers in each age band							Total numbers (thousands)
	Classroom teachers' pay spine [1]				Deputy heads	Heads	Total	
	0 - 8.5	9	9.5 - 13.5	14 - 17				
Nursery & Primary								
Under 25	99.9	-	-	-	-	-	100	10.4
25-29	83.2	10.2	5.6	-	0.9	0.1	100	28.1
30-34	28.9	24.8	35.2	0.1	9.2	1.9	100	20.7
35-39	24.3	22.5	33.1	0.1	12.9	7.0	100	15.7
40-44	13.3	25.2	36.4	0.2	12.3	12.6	100	26.0
45-49	4.1	26.1	40.3	0.2	12.3	17.0	100	40.1
50-54	1.7	24.1	40.0	0.3	11.4	22.5	100	29.3
55-59	0.8	21.3	38.5	0.3	11.5	27.6	100	9.6
60 and over	0.4	18.2	34.9	0.3	10.3	35.9	100	1.4
All ages	26.9	21.0	30.8	0.2	9.4	11.8	100	181.3
Secondary								
Under 25	99.9	0.1	-	-	-	-	100	6.7
25-29	82.3	9.2	8.5	-	-	-	100	26.2
30-34	33.6	17.3	47.2	1.5	0.4	-	100	21.3
35-39	13.3	15.2	63.9	4.3	2.8	0.4	100	20.8
40-44	5.6	14.9	67.4	5.8	4.5	1.8	100	30.6
45-49	2.5	14.5	67.4	7.0	5.2	3.4	100	42.4
50-54	1.2	14.8	64.2	8.1	6.6	5.1	100	30.1
55-59	0.6	16.6	60.0	8.2	7.7	6.9	100	9.6
60 and over	0.7	21.8	55.8	6.8	6.6	8.2	100	1.7
All ages	21.4	14.0	53.5	4.9	3.8	2.3	100	189.3
Special								
Under 25	100.0	-	-	-	-	-	100	0.1
25-29	70.5	12.2	17.0	-	0.3	-	100	0.8
30-34	18.8	8.4	66.6	0.7	4.6	1.0	100	1.0
35-39	8.9	4.6	71.8	2.2	8.0	4.4	100	1.4
40-44	3.9	2.4	73.4	2.4	10.0	7.9	100	2.9
45-49	1.9	1.6	73.6	2.5	10.3	10.1	100	3.9
50-54	1.3	1.0	72.4	2.4	9.9	13.0	100	2.8
55-59	0.7	1.0	68.7	2.8	9.7	17.0	100	0.9
60 and over	0.9	3.7	60.2	3.7	7.4	24.1	100	0.1
All ages	8.5	3.0	68.6	2.2	8.8	8.9	100	14.1

Source: Database of Teacher Records.

1. Teachers not on a spine point are allocated to the nearest point according to their salary.

2. Provisional estimates.

33

TEACHERS PAY
Full-time classroom teachers March 1999[1]: salary bands and average salary by sector, sex and age

ENGLAND AND WALES

	£11,000 -14,999	£15,000 -18,999	£19,000 -22,999	£23,000 -26,999	£27,000 and over	Salary unknown	Total	Average salary (£)
Nursery and primary								
Men								
Under 25	60	850	10	-	-	-	920	15,780
25-29	80	2,250	820	110	10	-	3,270	18,140
30-34	30	820	1,060	880	140	-	2,920	21,450
35-39	20	420	730	860	160	-	2,180	22,430
40-44	10	210	620	1,100	220	-	2,160	23,600
45-49	10	90	870	1,720	390	-	3,070	24,350
50-54	-	30	540	1,110	270	-	1,960	24,620
55-59	-	-	130	270	80	-	490	24,850
60 and over	-	-	40	60	10	-	110	24,610
All ages	200	4,660	4,820	6,110	1,290	-	17,080	21,900
Women								
Under 25	310	8,880	70	-	-	-	9,260	15,850
25-29	360	15,430	7,480	1,010	70	-	24,350	18,600
30-34	80	2,950	6,270	5,610	670	10	15,590	22,160
35-39	90	2,320	3,720	3,780	600	10	10,510	22,070
40-44	110	2,240	6,980	7,280	910	20	17,530	22,730
45-49	40	910	10,230	12,930	1,490	30	25,640	23,590
50-54	20	210	6,660	9,680	1,210	10	17,790	23,920
55-59	-	20	1,980	3,260	480	10	5,750	24,160
60 and over	-	-	240	450	100	-	790	24,490
All ages	1,020	32,960	43,620	44,000	5,520	90	127,210	21,720
Men and Women	1,220	37,620	48,440	50,110	6,800	90	144,290	21,750
Secondary								
Men								
Under 25	160	1,780	20	-	-	-	1,960	15,710
25-29	250	5,820	2,580	560	110	-	9,320	18,540
30-34	60	2,070	2,810	2,670	1,720	-	9,330	22,740
35-39	40	780	1,840	3,280	3,670	-	9,600	25,170
40-44	10	430	1,970	4,240	6,450	-	13,090	26,280
45-49	10	260	2,400	6,050	10,440	-	19,170	26,820
50-54	10	100	1,700	4,080	7,510	-	13,390	27,070
55-59	-	10	600	1,110	2,010	-	3,730	27,080
60 and over	-	-	190	270	300	-	760	26,080
All ages	530	11,250	14,110	22,230	32,210	10	80,340	24,880
Women								
Under 25	220	4,230	50	-	-	-	4,510	15,790
25-29	350	10,310	4,740	1,030	140	-	16,560	18,610
30-34	60	2,230	3,680	3,800	2,000	-	11,780	22,970
35-39	40	930	2,170	3,830	3,450	-	10,420	24,850
40-44	40	680	3,180	6,040	5,640	10	15,590	25,400
45-49	20	350	4,120	7,960	7,130	20	19,590	25,640
50-54	10	100	2,660	5,610	4,820	10	13,210	25,760
55-59	-	10	900	1,980	1,640	10	4,540	25,860
60 and over	-	-	140	330	290	-	760	26,020
All ages	750	18,840	21,640	30,560	25,110	60	96,950	23,560
Men and Women	1,280	30,080	35,750	52,800	57,310	60	177,290	24,160
Nursery, primary and secondary								
Men	730	15,910	18,930	28,340	33,490	10	97,420	24,360
Women	1,770	51,800	65,260	74,570	30,620	140	224,160	22,520
Men and Women	2,500	67,710	84,190	102,910	64,120	150	321,570	23,080

Source: Database of Teacher Records.

1. Provisional data.

34

ENGLAND AND WALES   (thousands)

| | Position in March 1998 | | | | | | | | |
| | Head-teachers | Deputy head-teachers | Classroom teachers spine point | | | | Other [3] | Not in service [4] | Total |
			14 - 17	9.5 - 13.5	9	0 - 8.5			
Position in March 1999									
Headteachers	18.5	1.2	-	0.3	-	-	-	0.4	20.4
Deputy headteachers	0.6	13.0	-	1.7	0.3	0.2	-	0.4	16.2
Classroom teachers spine point									
14-17	0.1	-	0.1	-	-	-	-	-	0.2
9.5-13.5	0.1	0.8	-	45.4	5.2	1.2	-	2.0	54.6
9	-	0.1	-	2.1	25.5	4.4	-	3.2	35.4
0-8.5	-	-	-	-	0.4	40.4	0.1	13.1	54.1
All classroom teachers	0.3	1.0	0.1	47.6	31.1	45.9	0.2	18.3	144.4
Other [5]	-	-	-	-	-	-	0.1	0.1	0.3
Total	19.3	15.1	0.1	49.5	31.4	46.2	0.3	19.3	181.3

Percentage distribution of those in service in 1999 by their position in 1998

| 1999 | 1998 | | | | |
	Head-teachers teachers	Deputy head-teachers	Classroom & other	Not in service [3]	Total
Headteachers	91	6	2	2	100
Deputy headteachers	4	80	14	3	100
Classroom & other	-	1	86	13	100

Source: Database of Teacher Records.

1. Grossed up for those whose pay details are not yet available.
2. Provisional data.
3. Mainly teachers without qualified teacher status in 1998.
4. Not in full-time service in 1998.
5. Mainly teachers without qualified teacher status in 1999.

TEACHERS PAY
Pay spine changes of teachers in full-time service in maintained secondary schools at March 1999 [1,2]

ENGLAND AND WALES   (thousands)

	Head-teachers	Deputy head-teachers	Classroom teachers spine point				Other [3]	Not in service [4]	Total
			14 - 17	9.5 - 13.5	9	0 - 8.5			
Position in March 1999									
Headteachers	3.8	0.3	-	0.1	-	-	-	0.1	4.3
Deputy headteachers	0.1	6.0	0.4	0.3	-	-	-	0.1	6.9
Classroom teachers spine point									
14-17	-	0.1	7.3	1.5	-	-	-	0.1	9.1
9.5 -13.5	-	0.1	0.4	90.0	4.8	1.6	-	2.5	99.6
9	-	-	-	1.6	17.0	3.9	-	2.1	24.6
0-8.5	-	-	-	0.1	0.3	32.5	0.1	11.4	44.3
All classroom teachers	-	0.2	7.7	93.2	22.1	38.0	0.2	16.1	177.6
Other [5]	-	-	-	-	-	-	0.2	0.1	0.5
Total	4.0	6.5	8.2	93.6	22.1	38.1	0.4	16.4	189.3

Percentage distribution of those in service in 1999 by their position in 1998

1999	1998				
	Head-teachers	Deputy head-teachers	Classroom & other	Not in service[4]	Total
Headteachers	89	7	3	2	100
Deputy headteachers	1	87	10	2	100
Classroom & other	-	-	91	9	100

Source: Database of Teacher Records.

1. Grossed up for those whose pay details are not yet available.
2. Provisional data.
3. Mainly teachers without qualified teacher status in 1998.
4. Not in full-time service in 1998.
5. Mainly teachers without qualified teacher status in 1999.

TEACHERS PAY

36

Full-time teachers in maintained nursery, primary and secondary schools: School group by grade and classroom teacher spine point, March 1999 [1]

ENGLAND[2]

(percentages)

	School group[3]						Total
	1	2	3	4	5	6	
Heads	23	10	6	3	2	1	6
Deputy heads	10	10	6	4	4	3	6
Classroom teachers on spine point [4]							
0	-	-	-	-	-	-	-
0.5	-	-	-	-	-	-	-
1	-	-	-	-	-	-	-
1.5	-	-	-	-	-	-	-
2	4	5	4	3	3	3	4
2.5	-	-	-	-	-	-	-
3	4	5	5	4	4	4	4
3.5	-	-	-	-	-	-	-
4	4	5	4	3	3	4	4
4.5	-	-	-	-	-	-	-
5	3	4	4	3	3	3	4
5.5	-	-	-	-	-	-	-
6	3	4	4	3	3	3	3
6.5	-	-	-	-	-	-	-
7	3	3	4	3	3	3	3
7.5	-	-	-	-	-	-	-
8	3	3	3	3	3	3	3
8.5	-	-	-	-	-	-	-
9	20	20	18	12	13	14	16
9.5	2	1	1	1	1	1	1
10	13	14	15	10	9	10	12
10.5	1	1	1	1	1	-	1
11	4	10	15	15	14	13	13
11.5	-	-	1	1	1	1	1
12	-	1	5	14	12	11	7
12.5	-	-	-	1	1	-	-
13	-	-	1	11	14	13	6
13.5	-	-	-	1	1	-	-
14	-	-	-	3	5	5	2
14.5	-	-	-	-	-	-	-
15	-	-	-	-	-	1	-
15.5	-	-	-	-	-	-	-
16	-	-	-	-	-	-	-
16.5	-	-	-	-	-	-	-
17	-	-	-	-	-	-	-
Total	100	100	100	100	100	100	100

Source: Database of Teacher Records.

1. Provisional data.
2. School group information not available for Wales.
3. Group number of school that teachers are serving in.
4. Teachers not paid on a spine are allocated the nearest point according to their salary.

TEACHERS PAY

Full-time heads and deputy heads: 1994 to 1999, by sector and school group [1]

ENGLAND AND WALES
(thousands)

	1994	1995	1996	1997	1998	1999 [2]
Heads						
Nursery and primary						
School group						
1	6.9	7.0	6.9	6.8	6.6	6.3
2	11.0	10.8	10.8	10.6	10.5	10.2
3 - 6	3.1	3.2	3.3	3.4	3.5	3.7
Total	21.0	21.0	21.1	20.8	20.6	20.2
Secondary[3]						
School group						
1	0.1	0.2	0.2	0.2	0.3	0.3
2	0.4	0.4	0.4	0.4	0.4	0.3
3	0.5	0.5	0.5	0.5	0.5	0.5
4	0.9	0.9	0.9	0.9	0.8	0.8
5	1.9	1.8	1.8	1.8	1.8	1.7
6	0.6	0.6	0.6	0.6	0.6	0.7
Total	4.4	4.4	4.4	4.3	4.3	4.3
Deputy heads						
Nursery and primary						
School group						
1	4.1	3.8	3.8	3.5	3.3	3.3
2	10.8	10.5	10.1	9.9	9.6	9.4
3 - 6	3.2	3.3	3.2	3.2	3.3	3.4
Total	18.1	17.7	17.2	16.6	16.1	16.1
Secondary[3]						
School group						
1	0.1	0.1	0.1	0.1	0.1	0.1
2	0.4	0.4	0.4	0.3	0.3	0.3
3	0.6	0.5	0.5	0.5	0.5	0.5
4	1.6	1.5	1.5	1.4	1.3	1.3
5	4.5	4.1	3.8	3.5	3.3	3.2
6	1.4	1.4	1.4	1.4	1.4	1.4
Total	8.5	8.1	7.6	7.1	6.9	6.9

Source: Database of Teacher Records.

1. School group number on which salary is based.
2. Provisional 1999 estimates. Excludes those whose school group information is not yet available.
3. Excludes sixth form colleges.

TEACHERS PAY

38

Full-time teachers: spine point [1] distribution by sector, sex and length of service, March 1999 [2]

ENGLAND AND WALES

	Percentage of teachers in each length of service band							
	Classroom teachers' pay spine [1]				Deputy heads	Heads	Total	Total numbers (thousands)
	0 - 8.5	9	9.5 - 13.5	14 - 17				
Nursery and primary								
Men								
0 - 4 years	94.1	3.1	1.9	-	0.2	0.8	100	6.4
5 - 9 years	19.2	25.7	38.7	0.1	13.3	3.0	100	4.1
10 - 14 years	0.6	15.5	39.4	0.3	26.2	18.0	100	2.6
15 - 19 years	0.2	12.8	32.1	0.8	20.7	33.5	100	2.4
20 + years	0.1	8.3	23.9	0.5	18.2	48.9	100	14.4
Total	22.7	10.6	23.3	0.4	14.7	28.3	100	29.9
Women								
0 - 4 years	96.0	2.5	1.2	-	0.3	-	100	42.5
5 - 9 years	26.0	33.2	34.1	-	5.5	1.1	100	25.9
10 - 14 years	1.1	35.4	46.6	0.1	11.2	5.6	100	19.8
15 - 19 years	0.5	30.3	46.9	0.1	12.0	10.2	100	23.5
20 + years	0.4	21.4	44.6	0.2	13.1	20.3	100	39.7
Total	31.4	21.4	31.4	0.1	7.8	7.9	100	151.3
Men and Women	30.0	19.6	30.0	0.1	9.0	11.3	100	181.3
Secondary								
Men								
0 - 4 years	88.2	6.4	5.4	-	-	-	100	17.7
5 - 9 years	14.2	26.4	58.0	1.0	0.3	0.1	100	11.1
10 - 14 years	0.3	16.6	74.7	4.8	3.0	0.6	100	8.4
15 - 19 years	0.2	11.9	72.8	7.1	5.5	2.4	100	11.6
20 + years	0.2	7.4	65.1	11.3	8.9	7.0	100	39.4
Total	19.4	11.1	54.4	6.6	5.1	3.5	100	88.1
Women								
0 - 4 years	92.6	4.1	3.3	-	-	-	100	27.0
5 - 9 years	17.6	27.3	53.9	0.8	0.3	0.1	100	15.0
10 - 14 years	0.7	23.0	71.2	3.0	1.7	0.4	100	13.4
15 - 19 years	0.3	17.9	73.0	4.4	3.2	1.2	100	18.4
20 + years	0.2	12.6	71.3	6.7	5.8	3.4	100	27.3
Total	27.2	14.9	51.1	3.2	2.5	1.2	100	101.1
Men and Women	23.5	13.1	52.6	4.8	3.7	2.3	100	189.3
Special								
Men								
0 - 4 years	69.4	8.8	21.4	-	0.4	-	100	0.6
5 - 9 years	5.5	6.0	82.0	1.1	5.1	0.2	100	0.5
10 - 14 years	0.2	0.4	81.0	2.8	9.1	6.5	100	0.5
15 - 19 years	0.2	0.7	68.8	3.1	13.6	13.6	100	0.9
20 + years	0.2	0.2	54.5	4.0	16.0	25.1	100	2.2
Total	9.2	2.0	58.8	2.9	11.8	15.3	100	4.6
Women								
0 - 4 years	75.2	7.1	17.1	0.3	0.2	0.2	100	1.2
5 - 9 years	6.4	9.8	80.8	0.2	2.4	0.3	100	1.3
10 - 14 years	0.4	0.8	88.4	1.2	6.6	2.5	100	1.7
15 - 19 years	0.1	0.4	83.6	2.3	8.5	5.1	100	2.2
20 + years	0.2	0.2	75.1	2.4	10.6	11.5	100	3.1
Total	10.2	2.5	73.2	1.6	7.0	5.5	100	9.5
Men and Women	9.9	2.3	68.6	2.0	8.5	8.6	100	14.1

Source: Database of Teacher Records.

1. Teachers not on a spine point are allocated to the nearest point according to their salary.
2. Provisional data

39

TEACHERS PAY
Average salary of full-time teachers in the maintained nursery, primary, secondary and special sector; sector and grade by sex and age, March 1999 [1]

ENGLAND AND WALES

	Men				Women			
	Head	Deputy head	Classroom	Total	Head	Deputy head	Classroom	Total
Nursery and primary								
Under 25	-	-	15,780	15,770	-	-	15,850	15,850
25-29	27,870	27,510	18,140	18,340	27,500	27,280	18,600	18,660
30-34	30,130	28,060	21,450	22,690	30,320	28,140	22,160	22,740
35-39	31,790	28,420	22,430	24,860	31,130	28,460	22,070	23,200
40-44	32,290	28,740	23,600	27,240	31,680	28,410	22,730	24,090
45-49	32,880	28,990	24,350	28,510	31,900	28,530	23,590	25,070
50-54	33,490	29,130	24,620	29,680	32,370	28,670	23,920	25,670
55-59	34,350	29,200	24,850	30,810	32,950	28,910	24,160	26,230
60 & over	35,370	29,700	24,610	30,080	34,330	29,360	24,490	27,060
all ages	33,070	28,780	21,900	26,070	32,120	28,500	21,720	23,070
Maintained secondary								
Under 25	-	-	15,710	15,710	-	-	15,790	15,790
25-29	-	27,640	18,540	18,540	-	29,800	18,610	18,610
30-34	29,560	34,450	22,740	22,800	32,810	33,460	22,970	23,010
35-39	40,610	35,320	25,170	25,590	37,660	34,880	24,850	25,110
40-44	43,110	35,700	26,280	27,200	40,620	35,480	25,400	25,940
45-49	44,430	35,850	26,820	28,210	42,350	35,540	25,640	26,340
50-54	46,360	36,440	27,070	29,250	44,120	35,880	25,760	26,640
55-59	48,640	36,690	27,080	30,210	43,550	36,340	25,860	26,820
60 & over	49,850	37,480	26,080	29,050	50,480	35,500	26,020	27,180
all ages	45,700	36,060	24,880	26,170	42,700	35,570	23,560	24,070
Special								
Under 25	-	-	16,760	16,760	-	-	16,710	16,710
25-29	-	27,630	19,720	19,810	-	-	20,110	20,110
30-34	33,250	31,400	23,390	23,940	33,910	29,970	24,590	24,850
35-39	36,410	32,070	25,830	26,980	33,470	31,120	25,390	26,120
40-44	38,490	32,130	26,890	29,000	36,140	30,830	25,920	26,820
45-49	39,100	31,900	27,490	30,060	36,750	31,210	26,100	27,100
50-54	38,920	32,560	27,300	30,590	36,670	31,480	26,300	27,510
55-59	42,050	32,510	27,840	32,890	38,020	31,180	26,520	27,970
60 & over	40,960	31,050	26,680	30,740	40,290	30,820	27,910	29,960
all ages	39,150	32,120	26,290	28,890	36,650	31,130	25,440	26,430
All sectors								
Under 25	-	-	15,730	15,730	-	-	15,840	15,840
25-29	25,910	27,520	18,460	18,510	26,220	27,310	18,620	18,660
30-34	30,140	28,680	22,460	22,800	30,500	28,330	22,560	22,900
35-39	33,080	30,840	24,700	25,470	31,510	29,530	23,530	24,160
40-44	34,780	32,190	25,950	27,300	32,700	29,880	24,070	24,980
45-49	36,080	32,520	26,520	28,360	33,070	29,840	24,550	25,630
50-54	37,380	33,480	26,780	29,410	33,530	30,200	24,780	26,100
55-59	39,380	34,270	26,860	30,450	34,040	30,540	24,990	26,530
60 & over	41,670	35,180	25,930	29,320	35,980	31,230	25,370	27,250
all ages	36,610	32,420	24,420	26,250	33,210	29,780	22,620	23,580

CONTINUED
TEACHERS PAY

39 Average salary of full-time teachers in the maintained nursery, primary, secondary and special sector; sector and grade by sex and age, March 1999 [1]

ENGLAND AND WALES

	Men and Women			
	Head	Deputy head	Classroom	Total
Nursery and primary				
Under 25	-	-	15,850	15,850
25-29	27,630	27,340	18,540	18,630
30-34	30,250	28,120	22,050	22,730
35-39	31,420	28,450	22,130	23,540
40-44	31,930	28,490	22,820	24,610
45-49	32,310	28,660	23,670	25,680
50-54	32,850	28,800	23,990	26,430
55-59	33,490	28,970	24,210	27,000
60 & over	34,640	29,430	24,500	27,580
all ages	32,510	28,570	21,750	23,570
Maintained secondary				
Under 25	-	-	15,760	15,760
25-29	-	28,720	18,580	18,590
30-34	31,730	33,970	22,870	22,920
35-39	39,710	35,130	25,000	25,340
40-44	42,180	35,610	25,800	26,530
45-49	43,800	35,740	26,230	27,300
50-54	45,830	36,270	26,420	28,030
55-59	47,470	36,580	26,410	28,480
60 & over	49,990	36,680	26,050	28,160
all ages	44,870	35,890	24,160	25,060
Special				
Under 25	-	-	16,720	16,720
25-29	-	27,630	20,020	20,040
30-34	33,830	30,610	24,270	24,600
35-39	35,040	31,410	25,540	26,420
40-44	37,470	31,420	26,220	27,570
45-49	38,210	31,550	26,520	28,150
50-54	37,960	31,950	26,560	28,490
55-59	40,120	31,770	26,770	29,260
60 & over	40,570	30,940	27,580	30,210
all ages	38,080	31,570	25,680	27,230
All sectors				
Under 25	-	15,010	15,820	15,820
25-29	26,120	27,370	18,580	18,630
30-34	30,370	28,430	22,530	22,870
35-39	32,230	30,010	23,950	24,640
40-44	33,640	30,720	24,670	25,740
45-49	34,500	30,900	25,200	26,590
50-54	35,450	31,630	25,440	27,290
55-59	36,520	32,070	25,530	27,810
60 & over	38,350	32,760	25,570	28,010
all ages	34,820	30,800	23,170	24,430

Source: Database of Teacher Records.

1. 1999 data are provisional.

PROMOTIONS
Promotions to head teacher: 1994-95 to 1998-99 by grade [1], sector and sex

ENGLAND AND WALES

	March 94 to March 95	March 95 to March 96	March 96 to March 97	March 97 to March 98	March 98 to March 99 [2]
Promoted from classroom teachers:					
Nursery and primary					
Men	50	60	60	80	50
Women	250	280	310	390	270
All teachers	310	340	370	480	310
Secondary [3]					
Men	40	40	60	70	60
Women	30	40	40	80	60
All teachers	70	80	100	150	120
Promoted from deputy heads:					
Nursery and primary					
Men	480	500	480	550	290
Women	990	1,040	1,150	1,280	890
All teachers	1,460	1,540	1,630	1,830	1,180
Secondary [3]					
Men	210	250	260	270	180
Women	130	90	120	140	110
All teachers	340	340	380	420	290

Source: Database of Teacher Records.

1. Those recorded as classroom or deputy head as at 31 March of one year and as head at 31 March the following year.
2. March 1999 data are provisional.
3. Excludes sixth form colleges.

TEACHER SICKNESS ABSENCE

Full-time and part-time teacher sickness absence in calendar year 1999 by local education authority [1]

ENGLAND

	Full-time (or full-time plus part-time if figures combined, see footnotes)			Part-time		
	Number taking absence	Total number of days taken	Days taken as part of absences of more than 20 days	Number taking absence	Total number of days taken	Days taken as part of absences of more than 20 days
Darlington	390	2,380	1,240	30	450	380
Hartlepool	450	6,340	3,430	20	260	200
Middlesbrough	790	6,640	2,630	50	500	280
Redcar and Cleveland	810	8,320	4,000	90	1,990	1,600
Stockton on Tees	1,080	16,430	10,560	70	1,050	650
Durham	2,510	14,810	9,470	120	850	590
Northumberland	1,380	15,280	4,580	220	2,680	800
Gateshead	1,000	14,030	7,960	30	240	110
Newcastle upon Tyne	1,420	25,710	17,840	90	1,530	830
North Tyneside [2]	940	13,650	120	..	..	..
South Tyneside	720	9,150	4,750	10	10	-
Sunderland	1,600	18,950	11,000	80	690	370
North East [3]	**12,860**	**136,940**	**70,520**	**910**	**11,020**	**6,020**
Blackburn with Darwen	620	10,320	6,360	70	730	310
Blackpool	760	9,110	4,510	70	1,040	640
Halton	620	2,200	840	60	20	0
Warrington	900	9,050	4,780	140	790	420
Cheshire [4]	3,960	39,910	19,450	420	..	..
Cumbria [4]	2,290	21,460	10,300	300	..	..
Bolton	1,090	16,200	2,020	70	2,960	430
Bury	980	9,750	4,390	80	750	430
Manchester	3,110	25,350	280	280	1,180	10
Oldham [4]	1,500	16,830	8,200	120	..	..
Rochdale	1,050	8,830	4,450	120	1,290	480
Salford	1,330	17,220	5,800	40	570	290
Stockport	1,260	10,030	3,050	120	920	180
Tameside	1,110	12,240	5,600	70	1,170	790
Trafford	830	13,770	9,910	70	690	380
Wigan	1,560	17,940	9,970	170	3,320	1,560
Lancashire	4,050	42,920	22,000	450	3,410	1,210
Knowsley	980	10,890	5,100	50	560	350
Liverpool [4]	1,880	22,740	9,510	90	..	..
St Helens [2]	2,320	13,140	7,360	..	..	..
Sefton [2]	1,960	18,150	4,770	..	..	..
Wirral	1,770	21,000	9,740	270	3,040	1,750
North West [3]	**34,340**	**355,450**	**159,510**	**3,430**	**36,690**	**16,130**

CONTINUED
TEACHER SICKNESS ABSENCE
Full-time and part-time teacher sickness absence in calendar year 1999 by local education authority [1]

ENGLAND

	Full-time (or full-time plus part-time if figures combined, see footnotes)			Part-time		
	Number taking absence	Total number of days taken	Days taken as part of absences of more than 20 days	Number taking absence	Total number of days taken	Days taken as part of absences of more than 20 days
East Riding of Yorkshire [5]	1,630	19,240	7,800	..	..	..
City of Kingston Upon Hull	1,370	14,870	6,670	140	1,430	830
North East Lincolnshire	900	9,210	4,040	80	880	310
North Lincolnshire	840	8,550	3,880	80	700	370
York	540	2,490	530	70	280	120
North Yorkshire [2]	3,600	49,560	21,140	..	..	..
Barnsley	4,050	42,920	22,000	450	3,410	1,210
Doncaster	1,630	17,040	8,090	130	1,520	910
Rotherham [6]	..	..	..	..	..	..
Sheffield	2,500	29,420	15,100	500	4,630	2,180
Bradford	2,650	33,540	18,280	160	2,700	1,690
Calderdale	790	7,830	3,790	90	790	350
Kirklees	2,210	24,780	11,300	300	3,170	1,520
Leeds	3,260	37,820	16,380	330	3,250	1,320
Wakefield	1,720	21,650	12,260	70	810	430
Yorkshire and The Humber [3]	**25,950**	**299,860**	**140,880**	**2,690**	**27,220**	**13,120**
Derby [2]	900	9,030	250	..	..	..
Leicester	1,990	17,840	7,750	250	1,420	450
Nottingham	1,450	14,620	6,660	220	1,220	370
Rutland	60	460	230	..	..	..
Derbyshire	3,000	35,220	19,040	580	6,800	3,910
Leicestershire	1,970	20,470	13,200	470	7,610	5,780
Lincolnshire [7]	..	26,720	3,520	..	..	..
Northamptonshire	3,510	26,960	13,030	300	2,810	1,030
Nottinghamshire [6]	..	..	..	..	..	..
East Midlands [3]	**18,200**	**184,370**	**78,460**	**2,670**	**27,240**	**13,860**
Herefordshire	720	5,980	2,350	170	1,070	410
Stoke on Trent [2]	1,370	19,470	11,540	..	..	..
Telford and Wrekin [1]	..	..	..	..	..	..
Shropshire	1,090	9,450	3,970	180	1,160	520
Staffordshire	3,620	44,800	24,300	350	2,410	750
Warwickshire [2]	3,350	27,880	10,100	..	..	..
Birmingham [6]	..	..	..	..	..	..
Coventry	2,450	21,270	9,560	230	3,470	2,080
Dudley	1,640	18,800	4,760	180	1,710	580
Sandwell [4]	2,070	22,480	9,200	230	..	..
Solihull	1,420	8,450	3,500	90	520	160
Walsall	1,420	16,890	8,830	70	790	440
Wolverhampton	1,420	10,850	5,550	160	800	220
Worcestershire	2,640	23,850	9,630	350	2,310	980
West Midlands [3]	**27,770**	**275,070**	**123,030**	**3,090**	**24,280**	**10,100**

TEACHER SICKNESS ABSENCE

Full-time and part-time teacher sickness absence in calendar year 1999 by local education authority [1]

41

ENGLAND

	Full-time (or full-time plus part-time if figures combined, see footnotes)			Part-time		
	Number taking absence	Total number of days taken	Days taken as part of absences of more than 20 days	Number taking absence	Total number of days taken	Days taken as part of absences of more than 20 days
Luton	620	7,410	2,530	150	940	380
Peterborough	600	6,840	3,650	130	2,240	1,640
Southend on Sea	920	8,390	3,260	100	540	80
Thurrock	810	7,670	2,270	60	550	350
Bedfordshire	1,930	16,500	6,820	330	1,680	590
Cambridgeshire	1,650	14,040	5,950	290	2,380	1,230
Essex	6,480	57,790	22,770	970	4,780	1,670
Hertfordshire	4,240	38,620	16,960	1,270	11,710	5,270
Norfolk	3,870	32,170	5,510	750	6,260	1,070
Suffolk	3,210	36,050	18,530	640	7,060	4,150
East of England [3]	**22,030**	**208,230**	**89,350**	**4,140**	**33,540**	**16,110**
Camden	1,020	4,860	1,670	150	590	210
City of London	10	90	..	..	40	30
Hackney	1,060	10,920	3,840	120	1,270	420
Hammersmith and Fulham	660	5,080	1,650	120	760	240
Haringey	1,060	8,320	2,970	150	1,780	1,010
Islington [2]	910	6,100	460	..	..	..
Kensington and Chelsea	410	3,260	1,040	90	490	..
Lambeth	1,090	7,630	2,130	230	1,750	80
Lewisham	770	5,120	2,040	170	1,560	520
Newham	1,910	22,700	11,300	70	1,870	1,330
Southwark	1,170	8,510	2,440	110	430	120
Tower Hamlets	1,500	13,900	4,720	190	1,690	710
Wandsworth	1,130	9,880	3,640	180	910	240
City of Westminster	750	1,890	640	130	930	60
Barking and Dagenham	970	7,900	2,820	80	580	310
Barnet	1,190	10,650	4,010	320	3,620	2,110
Bexley	1,350	11,680	4,560	120	930	440
Brent	1,550	13,800	4,920	60	540	170
Bromley [8]	960	5,890	..	80	610	..
Croydon	1,880	16,080	6,860	260	1,160	120
Ealing	1,710	12,940	4,010	170	900	190
Enfield	1,520	4,050	80	210	470	10
Greenwich	1,430	10,060	3,490	210	1,260	480
Harrow	1,080	10,150	3,610	210	1,850	790
Havering	430	2,380	220	50	110	-
Hillingdon	1,420	10,120	2,800	130	500	100
Hounslow	1,400	12,070	5,380	110	680	280
Kingston upon Thames	660	5,060	1,640	110	970	510
Merton [2]	470	5,680	2,460	..	..	..
Redbridge	1,040	9,430	3,560	160	1,240	550
Richmond upon Thames	510	3,770	1,140	80	350	10
Sutton	1,020	7,560	2,800	100	650	210
Waltham Forest [6]	..	..	..	..	..	..
London [3]	**35,100**	**284,470**	**101,360**	**4,510**	**33,180**	**12,330**

CONTINUED
TEACHER SICKNESS ABSENCE
Full-time and part-time teacher sickness absence in calendar year 1999 by local education authority [1]

ENGLAND

	Full-time (or full-time plus part-time if figures combined, see footnotes)			Part-time		
	Number taking absence	Total number of days taken	Days taken as part of absences of more than 20 days	Number taking absence	Total number of days taken	Days taken as part of absences of more than 20 days
Bracknell Forest	380	2,820	1,300	60	350	140
Brighton and Hove	310	6,000	4,580	20	140	70
Isle of Wight	680	6,410	2,960	100	560	230
Medway	1,130	12,090	6,420	150	1,770	1,110
Milton Keynes	600	4,380	1,310	30	220	30
Portsmouth	840	7,330	2,990	90	510	160
Reading	440	4,500	1,650	60	410	150
Slough	420	3,570	1,140	50	810	290
Southampton	1,160	11,260	4,750	110	670	240
West Berkshire	720	5,560	640	210	780	70
Windsor and Maidenhead	560	4,580	1,390	120	420	120
Wokingham [6]	..	..	..	..	..	..
Buckinghamshire	2,010	19,010	6,110	340	2,280	640
East Sussex [4]	2,230	14,460	4,070	330	..	..
Hampshire	5,840	50,760	22,230	710	4,610	1,720
Kent	6,220	51,230	19,720	710	4,560	1,560
Oxfordshire	420	7,830	5,740	480	9,360	6,900
Surrey	3,330	31,300	17,090	640	3,630	1,890
West Sussex [2]	5,320	34,860	13,620	..	..	..
South East [3]	**35,360**	**301,870**	**125,230**	**5,100**	**33,200**	**13,300**

41 TEACHER SICKNESS ABSENCE

Full-time and part-time teacher sickness absence in calendar year 1999 by local education authority [1]

ENGLAND

	Full-time (or full-time plus part-time if figures combined, see footnotes)			Part-time		
	Number taking absence	Total number of days taken	Days taken as part of absences of more than 20 days	Number taking absence	Total number of days taken	Days taken as part of absences of more than 20 days
Bath and North East Somerset	960	8,070	3,580	160	1,170	470
Bournemouth	780	8,540	4,660	120	1,070	550
City of Bristol	1,810	18,370	8,250	260	2,340	1,260
North Somerset [6]	..	..	..	..	..	..
Plymouth	1,140	10,370	3,910	120	970	170
Poole	450	4,230	1,450	60	430	110
South Gloucestershire	1,330	11,300	3,840	220	1,780	890
Swindon	1,040	9,070	3,930	90	580	280
Torbay	410	3,870	2,200	90	740	380
Cornwall	2,100	25,270	12,910	320	1,970	570
Isles of Scilly	10	180	140	..	40	40
Devon	2,650	30,020	16,080	480	5,210	2,860
Dorset	1,760	15,240	4,550	310	2,690	940
Gloucestershire	3,990	15,920	6,800	590	2,340	890
Somerset [6]	..	..	..	..	..	..
Wiltshire [6]	..	..	..	..	..	..
South West [3]	22,910	202,880	91,090	3,590	27,810	12,370
England [3]	234,520	2,249,150	979,440	30,130	254,180	113,350

Source: DfEE annual 618G survey.

1. Sickness absence on working days, whether paid absence or not, of teachers with permanent contracts or contracts of over one month. The number of teachers taking sick leave includes an individual teacher only once however many periods of sickness absence they have had. The number of days taken as sick leave includes all periods of sick leave.
2. Separate full-time and part-time figures not available. The combined full-time and part-time figures are shown in the full-time columns.
3. Regional and England totals have been grossed up for authorities that did not provide data or provided apparently inadequate data.
4. Separate full-time and part-time data only available for the number of teachers taking sickness absence. Combined full-time and part-time figures are shown in the full-time columns, the number of part-time teachers taking sickness absence is also shown.
5. Part-time sickness absence data not available.
6. Teacher sickness absence data not available.
7. Separate full-time and part-time data and number of teachers taking sickness absence is not available.
8. Breakdown of total sickness absence into periods of days not available.

VACANCIES

42

Vacancy numbers and rates in maintained nursery, primary and secondary schools, January 1995 to 2000: by local education authority [1] and Government Office region

ENGLAND AND WALES

	Number of vacancies						Vacancy rate(%)		
	1995	1996	1997	1998	1999	2000	1998	1999	2000
Gateshead	4	-	7	4	9	5	0.3	0.6	0.3
Newcastle upon Tyne	7	4	5	5	17	9	0.3	0.9	0.5
North Tyneside	-	-	-	-	26	15	-	1.8	1.1
South Tyneside	-	2	-	2	1	1	0.2	0.1	0.1
Sunderland	12	12	15	14	11	13	0.6	0.5	0.5
Former Cleveland	33	36	..	..	..	..	..	..	..
Hartlepool	..	..	7	4	9	3	0.5	1.2	0.4
Middlesbrough	..	..	4	11	6	4	0.9	0.5	0.3
Redcar and Cleveland	..	..	7	10	6	5	0.9	0.5	0.4
Stockton on Tees	..	..	12	9	7	6	0.6	0.5	0.4
Former Durham	6	12	6	..	..	..	..	..	..
Darlington	..	..	..	7	-	3	1.0	-	0.4
Durham (post 1.4.97)	..	..	..	18	2	2	0.5	0.1	0.1
Northumberland	-	-	-	-	-	-	-	-	-
NORTH EAST	**62**	**66**	**63**	**84**	**94**	**66**	**0.4**	**0.5**	**0.3**
Cumbria	2	3	4	2	2	-	0.1	0.1	-
Former Cheshire	24	29	21	39	..	..	0.5	..	..
Cheshire (post 1.4.98)	..	..	..	..	14	23	..	0.3	0.5
Halton	..	..	..	..	4	6	..	0.4	0.6
Warrington	..	..	..	..	7	11	..	0.5	0.7
Bolton	1	1	1	2	2	1	0.1	0.1	-
Bury	2	-	4	1	1	1	0.1	0.1	0.1
Manchester	8	2	7	-	-	-	-	-	-
Oldham	8	10	20	13	9	11	0.6	0.4	0.5
Rochdale	3	2	9	12	6	4	0.7	0.4	0.2
Salford	5	1	6	-	1	3	-	0.1	0.2
Stockport	4	7	1	-	5	6	-	0.3	0.3
Tameside	1	7	5	6	5	1	0.4	0.3	0.1
Trafford	1	1	3	2	1	-	0.1	0.1	-
Wigan	-	8	13	5	15	13	0.2	0.6	0.5
Former Lancashire	39	30	31	36	..	..	0.3	..	..
Lancashire (post 1.4.98)	..	..	..	..	30	21	..	0.4	0.2
Blackburn with Darwen	..	..	..	..	14	13	..	1.2	1.1
Blackpool	..	..	..	..	3	9	..	0.3	1.0
Knowsley	5	5	4	13	4	11	1.0	0.3	0.8
Liverpool	1	1	1	4	5	2	0.1	0.1	0.1
St Helens	1	6	8	5	5	1	0.3	0.4	0.1
Sefton	3	4	4	-	1	8	-	-	0.3
Wirral	5	4	7	14	17	10	0.5	0.6	0.4
NORTH WEST	**113**	**121**	**149**	**154**	**151**	**155**	**0.3**	**0.3**	**0.3**

42 VACANCIES

Vacancy numbers and rates in maintained nursery, primary and secondary schools, January 1995 to 2000: by local education authority [1]
and Government Office region
ENGLAND AND WALES

	Number of vacancies						Vacancy rate(%)		
	1995	1996	1997	1998	1999	2000	1998	1999	2000
Former Humberside	30	23	..	..	..	..	..	..	..
City of Kingston-Upon-Hull	..	..	2	1	1	-	0.1	0.1	-
East Riding of Yorkshire	..	..	-	1	4	2	-	0.2	0.1
North East Lincolnshire	..	..	-	2	-	-	0.2	-	-
North Lincolnshire	..	..	6	2	7	10	0.2	0.6	0.9
Former North Yorkshire	7	10	..	..	..	..	..	..	..
North Yorkshire (post 1.4.96)	..	..	-	16	8	9	0.4	0.2	0.2
York	..	..	-	-	7	6	-	0.6	0.5
Barnsley	-	-	1	7	2	2	0.5	0.1	0.1
Doncaster	1	-	-	-	-	2	-	-	0.1
Rotherham	-	-	-	-	1	1	-	-	-
Sheffield	7	14	13	20	2	6	0.6	0.1	0.2
Bradford	-	1	2	48	18	42	1.2	0.4	1.0
Calderdale	9	4	20	14	5	3	0.9	0.3	0.2
Kirklees	1	4	2	6	3	3	0.2	0.1	0.1
Leeds	26	13	10	25	7	18	0.5	0.1	0.3
Wakefield	1	-	-	-	-	2	-	-	0.1
YORKSHIRE AND THE HUMBER	**82**	**69**	**56**	**142**	**65**	**106**	**0.4**	**0.2**	**0.3**
Former Derbyshire	24	35	32	..	..	..	..	..	..
Derbyshire (post 1.4.97)	..	..	..	38	24	36	0.8	0.5	0.7
Derby	..	..	..	10	19	19	0.6	1.2	1.2
Former Leicestershire	13	22	32	..	..	..	..	..	..
Leicestershire (post 1.4.97)	..	..	..	11	13	13	0.3	0.3	0.3
Leicester City	..	..	..	12	11	20	0.6	0.5	0.9
Rutland	..	..	..	2	1	2	0.9	0.5	0.9
Lincolnshire	21	20	32	58	22	19	1.3	0.5	0.4
Northamptonshire	2	1	1	3	6	10	0.1	0.1	0.2
Former Nottinghamshire	1	8	-	-	..	..	-	..	..
Nottinghamshire (post 1.4.98)	..	..	..	..	-	-	..	-	-
City of Nottingham	..	..	..	..	-	24	..	-	1.3
EAST MIDLANDS	**61**	**86**	**97**	**134**	**96**	**143**	**0.5**	**0.3**	**0.5**

42 VACANCIES

Vacancy numbers and rates in maintained nursery, primary and secondary schools, January 1995 to 2000: by local education authority [1] and Government Office region

ENGLAND AND WALES

	Number of vacancies						Vacancy rate(%)		
	1995	1996	1997	1998	1999	2000	1998	1999	2000
Former Hereford and Worcester	-	3	4	7	..	..	0.1	..	..
Hereford (post 1.4.98)	..	..	..	..	6	11	..	0.5	1.0
Worcester (post 1.4.98)	..	..	..	..	11	6	..	0.3	0.2
Former Shropshire	3	3	3	1	..	..	-	..	..
Shropshire (post 1.4.98)	..	..	..	..	1	2	..	0.1	0.1
Telford & Wrekin	..	..	..	..	-	11	..	-	0.9
Former Staffordshire	28	19	26	..	..	..	..	..	..
Staffordshire (post 1.4.97)	..	..	..	21	21	27	0.4	0.4	0.5
Stoke	..	..	..	18	3	22	1.0	0.2	1.3
Warwickshire	1	4	10	12	14	13	0.4	0.4	0.4
Birmingham	10	24	32	37	71	60	0.4	0.8	0.7
Coventry	4	17	12	7	12	23	0.3	0.5	1.0
Dudley	9	7	8	14	7	16	0.6	0.3	0.7
Sandwell	15	8	20	15	28	15	0.6	1.1	0.6
Solihull	11	12	3	7	2	11	0.4	0.1	0.6
Walsall	26	16	8	36	12	8	1.6	0.5	0.4
Wolverhampton	6	6	9	8	33	10	0.4	1.7	0.5
WEST MIDLANDS	**113**	**119**	**135**	**183**	**221**	**235**	*0.5*	*0.5*	*0.6*
Former Cambridgeshire	3	13	6	7	..	..	0.1	..	..
Cambridgeshire (post 1.4.98)	..	..	..	..	1	-	..	-	-
Peterborough	..	..	..	..	2	-	..	0.1	-
Norfolk	14	27	30	30	55	30	1.1	1.1	0.6
Suffolk	16	25	30	22	31	19	0.5	0.6	0.4
Former Bedfordshire	1/	19	33	..	..	..	..	..	..
Bedfordshire (post 1.4.97)	..	..	..	23	24	39	0.8	0.8	1.4
Luton	..	..	..	23	24	14	1.6	1.7	1.0
Former Essex	105	66	78	102	..	..	0.9	..	..
Essex (post 1.4.98)	..	..	..	..	82	156	..	0.9	1.7
Southend	..	..	..	..	9	21	..	0.8	1.8
Thurrock	..	..	..	..	21	28	..	2.2	2.8
Hertfordshire	11	33	33	67	31	17	0.9	0.4	0.2
EAST OF ENGLAND	**166**	**183**	**210**	**274**	**280**	**324**	*0.7*	*0.7*	*0.9*

CONTINUED

VACANCIES

Vacancy numbers and rates in maintained nursery, primary and secondary schools, January 1995 to 2000: by local education authority [1] and Government Office region

ENGLAND AND WALES

	Number of vacancies						Vacancy rate(%)		
	1995	1996	1997	1998	1999	2000	1998	1999	2000
City of London	-	-	1	-	1	1	-	7.7	7.7
Camden	6	9	16	14	29	30	1.2	2.5	2.8
Greenwich	11	21	19	53	61	30	3.3	3.7	1.8
Hackney	38	23	24	60	68	69	4.8	5.3	5.3
Hammersmith & Fulham	5	7	24	47	23	22	6.1	3.0	2.8
Islington	7	15	17	42	13	31	3.6	1.2	2.7
Kensington & Chelsea	-	-	-	20	9	5	3.8	1.7	1.0
Lambeth	22	24	24	12	58	48	0.9	4.4	3.7
Lewisham	22	32	23	49	29	38	3.2	1.9	2.5
Southwark	8	11	24	60	61	72	3.9	4.0	4.6
Tower Hamlets	39	18	57	65	92	97	3.5	4.9	5.4
Wandsworth	9	22	29	34	29	23	2.5	2.1	1.7
Westminster	16	16	18	17	25	29	1.8	2.5	2.9
Barking and Dagenham	21	8	41	17	15	17	1.3	1.1	1.3
Barnet	21	20	15	22	32	49	1.0	1.4	2.2
Bexley	3	3	5	6	7	29	0.4	0.4	1.7
Brent	8	12	26	28	30	10	1.5	1.6	0.5
Bromley	5	13	11	15	13	12	0.8	0.6	0.6
Croydon	2	13	23	13	36	36	0.6	1.7	1.5
Ealing	15	18	23	47	54	32	2.5	2.8	1.6
Enfield	7	9	9	17	28	28	0.8	1.2	1.2
Haringey	4	27	42	30	33	33	1.9	2.1	2.1
Harrow	7	9	5	11	17	38	0.8	1.3	3.3
Havering	5	10	9	15	13	18	0.9	0.8	1.1
Hillingdon	32	18	19	28	27	23	1.6	1.5	1.2
Hounslow	5	13	14	22	15	8	1.3	0.9	0.5
Kingston upon Thames	4	7	3	6	9	8	0.7	1.0	0.9
Merton	-	-	8	7	11	16	0.7	1.1	1.6
Newham	60	74	99	82	37	54	4.0	1.7	2.5
Redbridge	3	6	4	17	14	7	0.9	0.7	0.4
Richmond upon Thames	2	6	3	3	4	15	0.3	0.5	1.8
Sutton	4	4	5	9	7	1	0.7	0.6	0.1
Waltham Forest	8	6	41	47	7	4	2.8	0.4	0.2
LONDON	**399**	**474**	**681**	**915**	**907**	**933**	**1.9**	**1.9**	**1.9**

VACANCIES

42 Vacancy numbers and rates in maintained nursery, primary and secondary schools, January 1995 to 2000: by local education authority [1] and Government Office region

ENGLAND AND WALES

	Number of vacancies						Vacancy rate(%)		
	1995	1996	1997	1998	1999	2000	1998	1999	2000
Former Berkshire	5	11	5	5	..	..	0.1	..	..
Bracknell Forest	..	..	..	..	-	9	..	-	1.4
Windsor	..	..	..	..	9	9	..	1.0	1.1
Newbury	..	..	..	..	2	4	..	0.2	0.3
Reading	..	..	..	..	2	14	..	0.2	1.8
Slough	..	..	..	..	18	13	..	2.0	1.5
Wokingham	..	..	..	..	14	14	..	1.3	1.3
Former Buckinghamshire	21	25	34	..	..	..	..	..	..
Buckinghamshire (post 1.4.97)	..	..	..	24	33	52	0.8	1.1	1.6
Milton Keynes	..	..	..	5	10	7	0.3	0.6	0.5
Former East Sussex	31	26	26	..	..	..	..	..	..
East Sussex (post 1.4.97)	..	..	..	29	22	23	1.0	0.8	0.8
Brighton & Hove	..	..	..	13	4	11	1.0	0.3	0.8
Former Hampshire	58	60	76	..	..	..	..	..	..
Hampshire (post 1.4.97)	..	..	..	57	93	142	0.7	1.2	1.8
Portsmouth	..	..	..	23	13	19	2.0	1.0	1.5
Southampton	..	..	..	19	15	25	1.3	1.0	1.8
Isle of Wight	1	-	-	-	-	1	-	-	0.1
Former Kent	86	104	94	89	..	..	0.8	..	..
Kent (post 1.4.98)	..	..	..	..	89	80	..	0.9	0.8
Medway	..	..	..	..	16	13	..	0.8	0.7
Oxfordshire	-	-	1	7	11	8	0.2	0.3	0.2
Surrey	21	15	37	41	20	37	0.7	0.3	0.6
West Sussex	19	23	37	39	17	38	0.8	0.4	0.8
SOUTH EAST	**242**	**264**	**310**	**351**	**388**	**519**	**0.7**	**0.8**	**1.0**
Former Avon	26	30	..	..	..	..	..	..	..
Bath & NE Somerset	..	..	3	5	4	4	0.4	0.3	0.3
City of Bristol	..	..	14	14	12	13	0.6	0.5	0.6
North Somerset	..	..	9	10	10	14	0.8	0.8	1.2
South Gloucestershire	..	..	10	7	4	3	0.4	0.2	0.2
Cornwall	1	2	9	8	6	11	0.2	0.2	0.3
Former Devon	21	15	22	22	..	..	0.3	..	..
Devon (post 1.4.98)	..	..	..	..	8	28	..	0.2	0.7
Plymouth	..	..	..	..	5	23	..	0.3	1.2
Torbay	..	..	..	..	3	7	..	0.4	0.9
Former Dorset	2	-	12	..	..	..	..	..	..
Dorset (post 1.4.97)	..	..	..	16	2	19	0.7	0.1	0.8
Poole	..	..	..	3	5	2	0.3	0.6	0.2
Bournemouth	..	..	..	-	1	2	-	0.1	0.2
Gloucestershire	7	10	14	8	9	25	0.2	0.2	0.6
Somerset	1	5	-	4	11	10	0.1	0.4	0.3
Former Wiltshire	14	12	19	..	..	..	..	..	..
Wiltshire (post 1.4.97)	..	..	..	18	21	14	0.7	0.8	0.5
Swindon	..	..	..	7	10	10	0.6	0.8	0.8
Isles of Scilly	-	-	1	-	-	-	-	-	-
SOUTH WEST	**72**	**74**	**113**	**122**	**111**	**185**	**0.4**	**0.4**	**0.6**

CONTINUED
VACANCIES

Vacancy numbers and rates in maintained nursery, primary and secondary schools, January 1995 to 2000: by local education authority [1] and Government Office region

ENGLAND AND WALES

	Number of vacancies						Vacancy rate(%)		
	1995	1996	1997	1998	1999	2000	1998	1999	2000
Clwyd	1	3	..	..	..	..	..	..	..
Dyfed	2	13	..	..	..	..	..	..	..
Gwent	2	-	..	..	..	..	..	..	..
Gwynedd	11	6	..	..	..	..	..	..	..
Mid Glamorgan	38	47	..	..	..	..	..	..	..
Powys	9	5	..	..	..	..	..	..	..
South Glamorgan	1	-	..	..	..	..	..	..	..
West Glamorgan	4	14	..	..	..	..	..	..	..
Anglesey	..	..	2	2	3	4	0.4	0.5	0.7
Gwynedd	..	..	3	6	5	2	0.6	0.5	0.2
Conwy	..	..	4	3	2	-	0.4	0.3	-
Denbighshire	..	..	-	2	1	-	0.3	0.1	-
Flintshire	..	..	10	4	3	2	0.4	0.3	0.2
Wrexham	..	..	8	1	9	7	0.1	1.0	0.8
Powys	..	..	6	10	9	-	1.0	0.9	-
Ceredigion	..	..	-	-	-	-	-	-	-
Pembrokeshire	..	..	-	11	3	3	1.1	0.3	0.3
Carmarthenshire	..	..	15	21	14	1	1.5	1.0	0.1
Swansea	..	..	6	4	10	3	0.2	0.5	0.2
Neath & Port Talbot	..	..	8	4	7	2	0.3	0.6	0.2
Bridgend	..	..	12	12	14	10	1.1	1.2	0.9
Vale of Glamorgan	..	..	-	11	12	7	1.1	1.2	0.8
Rhondda CT	..	..	9	41	20	15	1.9	0.9	0.7
Methyr Tydfil	..	..	-	1	-	-	0.2	-	-
Caerphilly	..	..	10	15	11	10	1.0	0.7	0.7
Blaenau Gwent	..	..	3	4	3	-	0.7	0.5	-
Torfaen	..	..	-	1	1	-	0.1	0.1	-
Monmouthshire	..	..	-	-	1	-	-	0.2	-
Newport	..	..	-	-	-	-	-	-	-
Cardiff	..	..	-	9	-	-	0.4	-	-
WALES	68	88	96	162	128	66	0.7	0.5	0.3
ENGLAND	1,310	1,448	1,814	2,359	2,313	2,666	0.7	0.7	0.8
ENGLAND AND WALES	1,378	1,536	1,910	2,521	2,441	2,732	0.7	0.7	0.7

Source: DfEE annual 618G survey and National Assembly for Wales stats3 survey.

1. The first, second and third phases of local government reorganisation came into effect on 1 April 1996, 1 April 1997 and 1 April 1998 respectively. The new authorities are shown directly below their former parent local authorities.

43

VACANCIES
Vacancy rates [1] in maintained nursery and primary schools January 1995 to 2000 [2], by grade and Government Office region

ENGLAND AND WALES

	Vacancies as a percentage of teachers in post [3]						Number of vacancies		
	1995	1996	1997	1998	1999	2000	1998	1999	2000
By grade:									
Head or deputy head	0.7	0.8	1.0	1.5	1.2	1.0	564	468	378
Head	0.5	0.6	0.7	1.0	0.9	0.8	223	195	164
Deputy head	0.9	1.1	1.3	2.0	1.6	1.3	341	273	214
Classroom teachers	0.4	0.4	0.5	0.6	0.6	0.7	929	956	1,067
By Government office region:									
North East	0.3	0.3	0.4	0.4	0.5	0.3	39	48	29
North West	0.3	0.3	0.3	0.3	0.3	0.3	91	92	75
Yorkshire and The Humber	0.3	0.2	0.1	0.4	0.2	0.3	69	42	49
East Midlands	0.2	0.4	0.4	0.5	0.4	0.6	77	51	83
West Midlands	0.3	0.2	0.2	0.4	0.7	0.6	80	135	124
East of England	0.5	0.6	0.7	0.7	0.8	0.9	133	147	165
London	1.0	1.2	1.7	2.5	2.3	2.0	625	589	520
South East	0.6	0.6	0.8	0.8	0.8	1.0	210	201	269
South West	0.3	0.3	0.5	0.4	0.4	0.7	67	69	106
England	0.5	0.5	0.6	0.8	0.8	0.8	1,391	1,374	1,420
Wales	0.3	0.3	0.5	0.8	0.4	0.2	102	48	25
England and Wales	0.4	0.5	0.6	0.8	0.8	0.8	1,493	1,422	1,445
Inner London Weighting Area	1.2	1.6	2.4	3.5	3.4	2.9	493	481	401
Outer London Weighting Area	0.6	0.7	0.9	1.1	0.9	1.0	132	108	119

Source: DfEE annual 618G survey and National Assembly for Wales stats3 survey.

1. Advertised vacancies for full-time permanent appointments (or appointments of at least one term's duration). Includes vacancies being filled on a temporary basis.
2. Excluding sixth form colleges.
3. Teachers in post include full-time regular teachers in (or on secondment from) maintained nursery and primary schools plus full-time regular divided service, peripatetic, advisory, remedial centres and miscellaneous teachers.

44

VACANCIES

Vacancy[1] rates in maintained secondary schools, January 1995 to 2000[2], by grade and Government Office region

ENGLAND AND WALES

	Vacancies as a percentage of teachers in post[3]						Number of vacancies		
	1995	1996	1997	1998	1999	2000	1998	1999	2000
By grade:									
Head or deputy head	0.5	0.6	0.7	1.0	1.0	0.9	114	114	106
Head	0.5	0.6	0.9	1.0	1.1	1.0	41	47	44
Deputy head	0.5	0.6	0.7	1.1	1.0	0.9	73	67	62
Classroom teachers	0.3	0.3	0.4	0.5	0.5	0.7	914	905	1,181
By Government office region:									
North East	0.3	0.3	0.3	0.4	0.5	0.4	45	46	37
North West	0.1	0.2	0.3	0.2	0.2	0.3	63	59	80
Yorkshire and The Humber	0.2	0.1	0.2	0.4	0.1	0.3	73	23	57
East Midlands	0.2	0.2	0.2	0.4	0.3	0.4	57	45	60
West Midlands	0.3	0.4	0.4	0.5	0.4	0.5	103	86	111
East of England	0.4	0.4	0.4	0.7	0.7	0.8	141	133	159
London	0.7	0.7	1.0	1.3	1.4	1.8	290	318	413
South East	0.3	0.5	0.5	0.6	0.7	1.0	141	187	250
South West	0.1	0.1	0.3	0.3	0.3	0.5	55	42	79
England	0.3	0.3	0.4	0.6	0.5	0.7	968	939	1,246
Wales	0.2	0.4	0.3	0.5	0.7	0.3	60	80	41
England and Wales	0.3	0.3	0.4	0.6	0.5	0.7	1,028	1,019	1,287
Inner London Weighting Area	1.1	0.9	1.6	1.7	1.8	2.3	191	197	256
Outer London Weighting Area	0.3	0.5	0.5	0.8	1.0	1.3	99	121	157

Source: DfEE annual 618G survey and National Assembly for Wales stats3 survey.

1. Advertised vacancies for full-time permanent appointments (or appointments of at least one term's duration). Includes vacancies being filled on a temporary basis.
2. Excluding sixth form colleges.
3. Teachers in post include full-time regular teachers in (or on secondment from) maintained secondary
   schools plus full-time regular divided service, peripatetic, advisory, remedial centres and miscellaneous teachers.

VACANCIES

Vacancy rates for classroom teachers in maintained secondary schools January 1995 to 2000 by subject

45

ENGLAND AND WALES

	Vacancies as a percentage of teachers in post [1,2]								Number of vacancies			
	1995	1996	1997 (old)	1997 (new)	1998	1999	2000	2000 (England only)	1998	1999	2000	2000 (England only)
Mathematics	0.2	0.2	0.4	0.4	0.7	0.8	1.2	1.2	141	155	239	233
Information technology	0.2	0.5	0.7	0.4	0.7	0.9	1.2	1.3	32	41	57	56
All Sciences [3] :	0.2	0.3	0.3	0.3	0.4	0.5	0.6	0.6	108	138	163	156
Chemistry	0.2	0.6	0.5	..	..	..	..	..	..	..	..	..
Physics	0.2	0.5	0.4	..	..	..	..	..	..	..	..	..
Biology	0.2	0.1	0.2	..	..	..	..	..	..	..	..	..
Other and combined science	0.2	0.2	0.3	..	..	..	..	..	..	..	..	..
Languages	0.4	0.5	0.6	0.5	0.7	0.5	0.7	0.7	120	89	112	109
English	0.3	0.3	0.4	0.4	0.5	0.4	0.6	0.7	109	88	133	129
Drama	0.3	0.3	0.5	0.4	0.2	0.4	0.6	0.7	8	14	23	23
History	0.1	0.2	0.1	0.1	0.2	0.2	0.1	0.2	20	18	12	12
Social sciences	-	0.1	0.3	0.2	-	0.1	0.2	0.2	-	4	8	8
Geography	0.3	0.3	0.3	0.3	0.4	0.1	0.3	0.3	32	11	29	25
Religious education	0.3	0.6	0.5	0.4	0.8	0.5	0.7	0.7	42	26	41	36
Design and technology [4]	0.3	0.2	0.3	0.3	0.7	0.6	0.7	0.7	111	101	111	110
Commercial / business studies	0.1	-	0.4	0.4	0.6	0.4	0.5	0.5	20	13	17	17
Art, craft or design	0.1	0.3	0.2	0.2	0.3	0.5	0.3	0.3	20	37	25	24
Home economics / needlework [4]	0.1	..	..	..	..	..	..	..	..	..	..	..
Music	0.7	0.3	0.8	0.9	0.7	0.7	0.8	0.8	30	32	36	35
Physical education	0.2	0.2	0.2	0.2	0.3	0.3	0.2	0.2	36	34	32	30
Special Educational Needs [5]	1.0	1.1	1.0	..	..	..	..	..	..	..	..	..
Careers	1.5	1.0	1.0	0.9	1.8	0.9	1.4	1.4	4	2	3	3
Other main and combined subjects [5]	0.6	0.6	0.9	0.7	0.7	0.8	1.1	1.2	81	100	140	137
Total classroom teachers	0.3	0.3	0.4	0.4	0.5	0.5	0.7	0.7	914	905	1,181	1,143

Source: DfEE annual 618G survey and National Assembly for Wales stats3 survey.

1. Teachers in post include full-time regular teachers in (or on secondment from) maintained secondary schools, plus the secondary portion of full-time regular divided service, peripatetic, advisory and miscellaneous teachers.
2. The number of teachers in post by main teaching subject is estimated using the 1992 Secondary School Staffing Survey for years 1995-1997 (old) and the 1996 Secondary Schools Curriculum and Staffing Survey for 1997 (new) to 2000.
3. Vacancies advertised in single sciences may be for combined science classes. The distinction between single science vacancies and combined science has been discontinued from 1997 (new).
4. From 1996, home economics / needlework is included with design and technology.
5. Special Educational Needs has been included in 'other main and combined subjects' from 1997 (new).

RETIREMENTS
Retirements from maintained nursery, primary, secondary and special schools [1]: Type of award and sex by year of award

ENGLAND AND WALES

	Premature [2]			Age			Ill-health [3]			Total		
	Men	Women	Men and Women	Men	Women	Men and Women	Men	Women	Men and Women	Men	Women	Men and Women
Financial year (1 April to 31 March)												
1989-90	3,540	5,250	8,780	990	2,570	3,550	1,280	2,330	3,600	5,800	10,140	15,940
1990-91	3,330	5,160	8,490	910	2,610	3,520	1,440	2,870	4,310	5,670	10,650	16,320
1991-92	2,720	4,390	7,110	830	2,370	3,190	1,410	2,650	4,060	4,960	9,400	14,360
1992-93	3,080	4,740	7,820	770	2,570	3,340	1,470	2,630	4,100	5,310	9,950	15,260
1993-94	3,470	5,210	8,680	870	2,590	3,470	1,870	3,020	4,890	6,220	10,820	17,040
1994-95	2,920	4,740	7,660	780	2,730	3,500	1,980	3,310	5,290	5,670	10,780	16,450
1995-96	3,530	5,550	9,080	740	2,710	3,450	1,880	3,310	5,190	6,150	11,570	17,720
1996-97 [2]	4,040	6,690	10,730	710	2,680	3,390	1,970	3,430	5,400	6,720	12,800	19,520
1997-98 [2]	4,780	7,820	12,600	790	2,830	3,620	1,350	2,290	3,640	6,930	12,930	19,860
1998-99	1,010	1,510	2,520	780	2,890	3,670	950	1,580	2,540	2,740	5,980	8,720
1999-00 [4]	1,200	1,620	2,820	910	3,170	4,080	900	1,570	2,470	3,010	6,350	9,370
(England only)												
1999-00 [4]	1,150	1,520	2,670	850	3,040	3,890	830	1,430	2,260	2,830	5,990	8,820

Source: Pensioner Statistical System (PENSTATS).

1. Includes sixth form colleges to 1993-94.
2. The effect of the change in the Teachers' Pension Scheme as from 31 August 1997 was that many more teachers took early retirement in 1997 than in previous years. This meant there was an increase of advertised teacher vacancies in 1996-97 and 1997-98
3. Changes in the statutory regulations governing ill-health retirement came into force on 1 April 1997. To qualify for ill-health retirement benefits a teacher must now be regarded as permanently unfit to teach.
4. 1999-00 data are provisional.

RETIREMENTS

Retirements: Type of award by last known sector [1] of service and sex: 1999-00 [2]

47a

ENGLAND AND WALES

	Premature	Age	Ill-health	Total
Nursery and primary				
Men	250	190	300	730
Women	900	1,610	970	3,480
Total	1,150	1,800	1,270	4,220
Secondary				
Men	910	690	560	2,150
Women	670	1,440	520	2,620
Total	1,580	2,120	1,070	4,770
Special				
Men	40	40	50	130
Women	50	120	80	260
Total	100	160	130	380
Nursery, primary, secondary and special				
Men	1,200	910	900	3,010
Women	1,620	3,170	1,570	6,350
Total	2,820	4,080	2,470	9,370
Other sectors [3]				
Men	200	960	320	1,480
Women	140	940	270	1,350
Total	340	1,900	580	2,830
Total				
Men	1,400	1,880	1,220	4,490
Women	1,760	4,100	1,840	7,700
Total	3,160	5,980	3,050	12,190

Source: Pensioner Statistical System (PENSTATS).

1. The last known sector of a teacher may have been some years prior to retirement date.
2. Provisional data.
3. Including those from independent schools and further and higher education establishments covered by the Teachers Pension Scheme.

RETIREMENTS

47b

Retirements: Type of award by last known sector [1] of service and sex: 1999-00 [2]

ENGLAND ONLY

	Premature	Age	Ill-health	Total
Nursery and primary				
Men	230	180	270	680
Women	860	1,550	880	3,280
Total	1,090	1,730	1,150	3,970
Secondary				
Men	870	640	520	2,020
Women	620	1,370	480	2,460
Total	1,490	2,010	990	4,490
Special				
Men	40	30	40	120
Women	50	120	80	250
Total	100	150	120	370
Nursery, primary, secondary and special				
Men	1,150	850	830	2,830
Women	1,520	3,040	1,430	5,990
Total	2,670	3,890	2,260	8,820
Other sectors [3]				
Men	180	940	300	1,420
Women	130	920	260	1,310
Total	320	1,860	550	2,730
Total				
Men	1,330	1,790	1,130	4,250
Women	1,660	3,960	1,690	7,300
Total	2,990	5,740	2,820	11,550

Source: Pensioner Statistical System (PENSTATS).

1. The last known sector of a teacher may have been some years prior to retirement date.
2. Provisional data.
3. Including those from independent schools and further and higher education establishments covered by the Teachers Pension Scheme.

RETIREMENTS

48a

Retirements: Type of award by last known sector[1] of service and grade: 1999-00[2]

ENGLAND AND WALES

	Premature	Age	Ill-health	Total
Nursery and primary				
Head teachers	250	270	210	720
Deputy heads	130	140	130	400
Classroom teachers	770	1,380	930	3,080
Others	10	10	-	20
Total	1,150	1,800	1,270	4,220
Secondary				
Head teachers	100	70	30	200
Deputy heads	120	80	30	230
Classroom teachers	1,350	1,950	1,010	4,300
Others	10	30	10	50
Total	1,580	2,120	1,070	4,770
Special				
Head teachers	20	10	10	40
Deputy heads	10	10	10	30
Classroom teachers	70	140	110	310
Others	-	-	-	-
Total	100	160	130	380
Nursery, primary, secondary and special schools				
Head teachers	360	360	240	960
Deputy heads	260	220	170	650
Classroom teachers	2,180	3,470	2,040	7,690
Others	20	30	10	70
Total	2,820	4,080	2,470	9,370
Other sectors[3]				
Head teachers	-	-	-	-
Deputy heads	10	-	-	10
Classroom teachers	330	1,890	580	2,800
Others	-	-	-	10
Total	340	1,900	580	2,820
Total				
Head teachers	360	360	250	970
Deputy heads	270	230	170	670
Classroom teachers	2,510	5,360	2,620	10,490
Others	20	40	20	70
Total	3,160	5,980	3,050	12,190

Source: Database of Teacher Records and Pensioner Statistical System (PENSTATS).

1. The last known sector of a teacher may have been some years prior to retirement date.
2. Provisional data.
3. Including those from independent schools and further and higher education establishments covered by the Teachers Pension Scheme.

RETIREMENTS

Retirements: Type of award by last known sector[1] of service and grade: 1999-00[2]

ENGLAND ONLY

	Premature	Age	Ill-health	Total
Nursery and primary				
Head teachers	230	260	180	670
Deputy heads	130	130	120	380
Classroom teachers	730	1,330	850	2,900
Others	10	10	-	20
Total	1,090	1,730	1,150	3,970
Secondary				
Head teachers	100	70	30	190
Deputy heads	110	70	20	200
Classroom teachers	1,270	1,850	930	4,050
Others	10	30	10	40
Total	1,490	2,010	990	4,490
Special				
Head teachers	20	10	10	40
Deputy heads	10	10	-	30
Classroom teachers	70	130	110	300
Others	-	-	-	-
Total	100	150	120	370
Nursery, primary, secondary and special schools				
Head teachers	350	330	220	900
Deputy heads	250	210	150	600
Classroom teachers	2,060	3,310	1,890	7,260
Others	20	30	10	60
Total	2,670	3,890	2,260	8,820
Other sectors[3]				
Head teachers	-	-	-	-
Deputy heads	10	-	-	10
Classroom teachers	310	1,850	550	2,700
Others	-	-	-	10
Total	320	1,860	550	2,730
Total				
Head teachers	350	340	220	900
Deputy heads	260	210	150	620
Classroom teachers	2,370	5,160	2,430	9,960
Others	20	40	10	70
Total	2,990	5,740	2,820	11,550

Source: Database of Teacher Records and Pensioner Statistical System (PENSTATS).

1. The last known sector of a teacher may have been some years prior to retirement date.
2. Provisional data.
3. Including those from independent schools and further and higher education establishments covered by the Teachers Pension Scheme.

49a

RETIREMENTS

Retirements from maintained nursery, primary, secondary and special schools: Type of award by sex and age on retirement: 1999-00[1]

ENGLAND AND WALES

	Premature	Age	Ill-health	Total
Men				
Under 30	-	-	-	-
30-34	-	-	10	10
35-39	-	-	20	20
40-44	-	-	60	60
45-49	-	-	250	250
50-54	660	-	400	1,050
55-59	510	-	160	680
60-64	30	840	-	880
65 & over	-	70	-	70
all ages	1,200	910	900	3,010
Women				
Under 30	-	-	-	-
30-34	-	-	20	20
35-39	-	-	30	30
40-44	-	-	90	90
45-49	-	-	390	390
50-54	690	-	630	1,320
55-59	860	10	400	1,280
60-64	70	3,040	-	3,120
65 & over	-	110	-	110
all ages	1,620	3,170	1,570	6,350
Men and women				
Under 30	-	-	-	-
30-34	-	-	20	20
35-39	-	-	50	50
40-44	-	-	160	160
45-49	-	-	640	640
50-54	1,340	-	1,030	2,370
55-59	1,370	20	570	1,950
60-64	100	3,880	10	3,990
65 & over	-	180	-	180
all ages	2,820	4,080	2,470	9,370

Source: Database of Teacher Records and Pensioner Statistical System (PENSTATS).

1. 1999-00 data are provisional.

RETIREMENTS

Retirements from maintained nursery, primary, secondary and special schools: Type of award by sex and age on retirement: 1999-00[1]

ENGLAND ONLY

	Premature	Age	Ill-health	Total
Men				
Under 30	-	-	-	-
30-34	-	-	10	10
35-39	-	-	10	10
40-44	-	-	50	50
45-49	-	-	240	240
50-54	640	-	370	1,000
55-59	480	-	150	630
60-64	30	780	-	820
65 & over	-	60	-	70
all ages	1,150	850	830	2,830
Women				
Under 30	-	-	-	-
30-34	-	-	10	10
35-39	-	-	30	30
40-44	-	-	90	90
45-49	-	-	360	360
50-54	640	-	570	1,210
55-59	810	10	370	1,200
60-64	70	2,920	-	2,990
65 & over	-	110	-	110
all ages	1,520	3,040	1,430	5,990
Men and women				
Under 30	-	-	-	-
30-34	-	-	20	20
35-39	-	-	40	40
40-44	-	-	140	140
45-49	-	-	590	590
50-54	1,280	-	940	2,210
55-59	1,290	20	520	1,830
60-64	100	3,700	10	3,810
65 & over	-	170	-	180
all ages	2,670	3,890	2,260	8,820

Source: Database of Teacher Records and Pensioner Statistical System (PENSTATS).

1. 1999-00 data are provisional.

RETIREMENTS

Retirements from maintained nursery, primary, secondary and special schools: type of award and sex by year of retirement, new[1] and current[2] awards and average benefits[3] awarded

ENGLAND AND WALES

	Premature			Age		
	Men	Women	All	Men	Women	All
1996-97						
New[1] awards						
Number	4,040	6,690	10,730	710	2,680	3,390
Average benefits[3]	£9,800	£7,100	£8,100	£7,300	£4,600	£5,200
Current[2] awards	50,400	80,050	130,440	25,800	67,380	93,180
1997-98						
New[1] awards						
Number	4,780	7,820	12,600	790	2,830	3,620
Average benefits[3]	£9,900	£7,100	£8,100	£8,400	£5,100	£5,800
Current[2] awards	54,510	87,330	141,840	25,180	67,580	92,760
1998-99[4]						
New[1] awards						
Number	1,010	1,510	2,520	780	2,890	3,670
Average benefits[3]	£7,890	£5,690	£6,570	£8,710	£5,210	£5,950
Current[2] awards	54,820	88,220	143,030	24,570	67,870	92,440
1999-00[4]						
New[1] awards						
Number	1,200	1,620	2,870	910	3,170	4,080
Average benefits[3]	£8,340	£5,980	£6,980	£9,000	£5,630	£6,390
Current[2] awards	54,150	87,660	141,810	23,240	65,790	89,030
1999-00 England only[4]						
New[1] awards						
Number	1,150	1,520	2,670	850	3,040	3,890
Average benefits[3]	£8,300	£5,980	£6,970	£8,790	£5,600	£6,300
Current[2] awards	50,370	81,280	131,650	22,990	65,270	88,260

RETIREMENTS

Retirements from maintained nursery, primary, secondary and special schools: type of award and sex by year of retirement, new[1] and current[2] awards and average benefits[3] awarded - Continued

ENGLAND AND WALES

	Ill-health			Total		
	Men	Women	All	Men	Women	All
1996-97						
New[1] awards						
Number	1,970	3,430	5,400	6,720	12,800	19,520
Average benefits[3]	£9,700	£7,500	£8,300	£9,500	£6,700	£7,700
Current[2] awards	19,930	36,730	56,650	96,120	184,150	280,280
1997-98						
New[1] awards						
Number	1,350	2,290	3,640	6,930	12,930	19,860
Average benefits[3]	£10,000	£7,800	£8,600	£9,700	£6,800	£7,800
Current[2] awards	20,990	38,610	59,600	100,680	193,520	294,200
1998-99[4]						
New[1] awards						
Number	950	1,580	2,540	2,740	5,980	8,720
Average benefits[3]	£10,280	£7,900	£8,800	£8,950	£6,040	£6,960
Current[2] awards	21,660	39,730	61,390	101,040	195,820	296,860
1999-00[4]						
New[1] awards						
Number	900	1,570	2,470	3,010	6,350	9,370
Average benefits[3]	£10,630	£8,350	£9,180	£9,220	£6,390	£7,300
Current[2] awards	21,500	39,740	61,240	98,890	193,190	292,080
1999-00 England only[4]						
New[1] awards						
Number	830	1,430	2,260	2,830	5,990	8,820
Average benefits[3]	£10,610	£8,320	£9,160	£9,130	£6,340	£7,240
Current[2] awards	21,000	38,960	59,960	94,360	185,510	279,870

Source: Database of Teacher Records and Pensioner Statistical System (PENSTATS).

1. 'New' is defined as those awarded retirement benefits in the financial year shown.
2. 'Current' includes teachers awarded retirement benefits in the current financial year plus those awarded benefits in a previous financial year and who are still receiving benefits up to the end of the year shown.
3. This is the average of the annual pension and does not include the one-off 'lump-sum' payments.
4. Provisional data.

OUT OF SERVICE TEACHERS AGED UNDER 60

Qualified teachers out of service [1,2] at 31 March 1999 aged under 60 who were previously in service , by last known sector, calendar year of last service, sex and age at 31 March 1999 [3]

ENGLAND AND WALES   (thousands)

	Nursery and primary					Secondary					Special				
	Calendar year of last service					Calendar year of last service					Calendar year of last service				
	before 1983	1983 to 1987	1988 to 1992	1993 to 1999	all years	before 1983	1983 to 1987	1988 to 1992	1993 to 1999	all years	before 1983	1983 to 1987	1988 to 1992	1993 to 1999	all years
Men															
Under 25	-	-	-	-	-	-	-	-	0.1	0.1	-	-	-	-	-
25-29	-	-	-	0.5	0.5	-	-	-	1.6	1.6	-	-	-	-	-
30-34	-	-	0.1	0.8	0.9	-	-	0.4	2.4	2.9	-	-	-	0.1	0.1
35-39	-	0.1	0.4	0.7	1.1	-	0.9	1.5	2.0	4.3	-	-	-	0.1	0.2
40-44	0.1	0.2	0.3	0.6	1.2	1.3	2.5	1.4	1.8	7.0	-	0.1	0.1	0.1	0.3
45-49	0.8	0.3	0.4	0.8	2.3	6.6	2.2	1.8	2.4	13.0	0.1	0.1	0.1	0.2	0.5
50-54	1.8	0.3	0.5	0.7	3.2	10.2	1.8	1.9	2.1	16.0	0.2	0.1	0.1	0.1	0.5
55-59	1.7	0.2	0.3	0.2	2.4	8.7	0.9	0.9	0.8	11.3	0.2	-	0.1	-	0.3
Total	4.4	1.1	1.9	4.3	11.8	26.8	8.4	7.9	13.3	56.3	0.5	0.3	0.4	0.7	1.9
Women															
Under 25	-	-	-	0.4	0.4	-	-	-	0.2	0.2	-	-	-	-	-
25-29	-	-	-	4.4	4.4	-	-	-	3.6	3.6	-	-	-	0.1	0.1
30-34	-	-	1.2	7.0	8.2	-	-	0.9	5.4	6.3	-	-	-	0.2	0.3
35-39	-	0.7	3.1	5.1	8.9	-	1.4	3.0	4.8	9.2	-	0.1	0.1	0.3	0.5
40-44	1.2	1.9	2.3	3.8	9.2	2.5	4.0	2.9	4.9	14.3	0.1	0.3	0.2	0.3	0.9
45-49	7.6	1.9	2.7	4.8	16.9	10.5	3.2	2.9	5.6	22.2	0.5	0.2	0.2	0.4	1.3
50-54	13.7	1.6	2.6	4.3	22.3	15.8	2.6	2.9	5.1	26.4	0.7	0.1	0.2	0.3	1.4
55-59	11.7	1.2	1.9	2.0	16.7	15.1	1.9	2.1	2.6	21.8	0.5	0.1	0.1	0.2	0.9
Total	34.2	7.2	13.9	31.7	87.0	43.9	13.1	14.7	32.3	103.9	1.8	0.8	0.9	1.9	5.4
Men and women															
Under 25	-	-	-	0.4	0.4	-	-	-	0.3	0.3	-	-	-	-	-
25-29	-	-	-	4.9	4.9	-	-	-	5.3	5.3	-	-	-	0.1	0.1
30-34	-	-	1.4	7.8	9.1	-	-	1.3	7.9	9.1	-	-	-	0.3	0.3
35-39	-	0.8	3.5	5.8	10.0	-	2.3	4.4	6.8	13.5	-	0.1	0.2	0.4	0.7
40-44	1.3	2.1	2.6	4.4	10.4	3.7	6.5	4.4	6.7	21.3	0.1	0.3	0.3	0.5	1.2
45-49	8.4	2.2	3.0	5.7	19.2	17.0	5.4	4.7	8.0	35.2	0.6	0.3	0.3	0.6	1.8
50-54	15.5	1.9	3.1	5.0	25.5	26.0	4.4	4.8	7.2	42.4	0.9	0.2	0.3	0.5	1.9
55-59	13.4	1.4	2.2	2.1	19.1	23.8	2.9	3.0	3.4	33.1	0.7	0.2	0.2	0.2	1.2
Total	38.6	8.4	15.8	36.0	98.8	70.6	21.5	22.5	45.5	160.2	2.3	1.0	1.3	2.6	7.2

CONTINUED
OUT OF SERVICE TEACHERS AGED UNDER 60

Qualified teachers out of service[1,2] at 31 March 1999 aged under 60 who were previously in service,
by last known sector, calendar year of last service, sex and age at 31 March 1999[3]
ENGLAND AND WALES (thousands)

| | Other[4] | | | | | Total | | | | |
| | Calendar year of last service | | | | | Calendar year of last service | | | | |
	before 1983	1983 to 1987	1988 to 1992	1993 to 1999	all years	before 1983	1983 to 1987	1988 to 1992	1993 to 1999	all years
Men										
Under 25	-	-	-	-	-	-	-	-	0.2	0.2
25-29	-	-	-	0.2	0.2	-	-	-	2.4	2.4
30-34	-	-	-	0.5	0.5	-	-	0.6	3.8	4.4
35-39	-	0.1	0.2	0.5	0.8	-	1.1	2.0	3.3	6.4
40-44	0.1	0.4	0.4	0.7	1.6	1.5	3.2	2.2	3.3	10.2
45-49	0.7	0.6	0.6	1.2	3.1	8.2	3.2	2.9	4.6	18.9
50-54	1.4	0.6	0.8	1.1	4.0	13.6	2.9	3.2	4.0	23.7
55-59	1.7	0.4	0.4	0.4	2.9	12.3	1.6	1.7	1.4	16.9
Total	4.0	2.1	2.4	4.6	13.2	35.7	11.9	12.6	23.0	83.1
Women										
Under 25	-	-	-	-	-	-	-	-	0.6	0.6
25-29	-	-	-	0.6	0.6	-	-	-	8.7	8.7
30-34	-	-	0.1	1.1	1.2	-	-	2.2	13.7	15.9
35-39	-	0.2	0.6	1.1	1.9	-	2.4	6.8	11.3	20.5
40-44	0.3	0.8	0.7	1.2	3.1	4.1	6.9	6.2	10.3	27.5
45-49	1.3	0.7	0.7	1.7	4.3	19.8	5.9	6.4	12.5	44.6
50-54	2.0	0.6	0.8	1.7	5.1	32.3	4.9	6.5	11.5	55.2
55-59	1.8	0.4	0.6	0.9	3.7	29.1	3.7	4.7	5.6	43.1
Total	5.4	2.7	3.4	8.4	19.9	85.3	23.8	32.9	74.2	216.2
Men and women										
Under 25	-	-	-	-	-	-	-	-	0.8	0.8
25-29	-	-	-	0.9	0.9	-	-	-	11.1	11.2
30-34	-	-	0.1	1.6	1.7	-	-	2.8	17.5	20.3
35-39	-	0.3	0.8	1.7	2.7	-	3.4	8.8	14.6	26.9
40-44	0.5	1.2	1.1	2.0	4.7	5.6	10.1	8.4	13.6	37.7
45-49	2.0	1.2	1.3	2.9	7.4	28.0	9.1	9.3	17.1	63.5
50-54	3.5	1.2	1.5	2.8	9.1	45.9	7.8	9.7	15.5	78.9
55-59	3.5	0.9	1.0	1.3	6.6	41.4	5.3	6.4	7.0	60.0
Total	9.4	4.8	5.8	13.0	33.1	121.0	35.7	45.4	97.2	299.3

Source: Database of Teacher Records.

1. Excluding those who are receiving a pension from the Teachers Pension Scheme (TPS).
2. Some in service teachers may be shown as not in service because their service details are not recorded. These may include qualified teachers in the 'old' university sector, teachers in the independent sector who are not members of the Teachers Pension Scheme (TPS), part-time teachers outside the maintained nursey, primary and secondary sector who are not members of the TPS.
3. Provisional data.
4. Other includes the independent sector, further and higher education.

OUT OF SERVICE TEACHERS AGED UNDER 60

Qualified teachers out of service[1,2] at 31 March 1999 aged under 60 who were previously in service , by last known sector, calendar year of last service, sex and age at 31 March 1999[3]

ENGLAND ONLY

(thousands)

	Nursery and primary					Secondary					Special				
	Calendar year of last service					Calendar year of last service					Calendar year of last service				
	before 1983	1983 to 1987	1988 to 1992	1993 to 1999	all years	before 1983	1983 to 1987	1988 to 1992	1993 to 1999	all years	before 1983	1983 to 1987	1988 to 1992	1993 to 1999	all years
Men															
Under 25	-	-	-	-	-	-	-	-	0.1	0.1	-	-	-	-	-
25-29	-	-	-	0.5	0.5	-	-	-	1.6	1.6	-	-	-	-	-
30-34	-	-	0.1	0.8	0.9	-	-	0.4	2.3	2.7	-	-	-	0.1	0.1
35-39	-	0.1	0.3	0.6	1.1	-	0.9	1.4	1.9	4.1	-	-	-	0.1	0.1
40-44	0.1	0.2	0.3	0.5	1.1	1.2	2.4	1.4	1.7	6.7	-	0.1	0.1	0.1	0.3
45-49	0.8	0.3	0.4	0.8	2.2	6.3	2.1	1.7	2.3	12.5	0.1	0.1	0.1	0.2	0.5
50-54	1.7	0.3	0.4	0.6	3.1	10.0	1.7	1.8	2.0	15.6	0.2	0.1	0.1	0.1	0.5
55-59	1.7	0.2	0.3	0.2	2.3	8.6	0.9	0.9	0.7	11.1	0.2	-	-	-	0.3
Total	4.3	1.1	1.8	4.1	11.2	26.2	8.0	7.5	12.6	54.4	0.5	0.3	0.3	0.7	1.8
Women															
Under 25	-	-	-	0.3	0.3	-	-	-	0.2	0.2	-	-	-	-	-
25-29	-	-	-	4.2	4.2	-	-	-	3.4	3.4	-	-	-	0.1	0.1
30-34	-	-	1.2	6.7	7.9	-	-	0.8	5.1	6.0	-	-	-	0.2	0.3
35-39	-	0.7	3.0	4.9	8.6	-	1.4	2.9	4.6	8.8	-	0.1	0.1	0.3	0.5
40-44	1.1	1.8	2.2	3.7	8.8	2.3	3.8	2.8	4.6	13.6	0.1	0.3	0.2	0.3	0.9
45-49	7.3	1.8	2.6	4.6	16.3	10.1	3.1	2.8	5.2	21.2	0.5	0.2	0.2	0.4	1.2
50-54	13.5	1.6	2.6	4.1	21.8	15.5	2.4	2.8	4.7	25.5	0.7	0.1	0.2	0.3	1.4
55-59	11.6	1.1	1.9	1.9	16.5	15.0	1.9	2.0	2.4	21.2	0.5	0.1	0.1	0.1	0.9
Total	33.6	7.0	13.4	30.4	84.4	43.0	12.6	14.1	30.2	99.9	1.8	0.7	0.9	1.8	5.3
Men and women															
Under 25	-	-	-	0.4	0.4	-	-	-	0.3	0.3	-	-	-	-	-
25-29	-	-	-	4.7	4.7	-	-	-	5.0	5.0	-	-	-	0.1	0.1
30-34	-	-	1.3	7.5	8.8	-	-	1.2	7.5	8.7	-	-	-	0.3	0.3
35-39	-	0.8	3.4	5.5	9.7	-	2.2	4.3	6.4	12.9	-	0.1	0.2	0.4	0.6
40-44	1.2	2.0	2.5	4.2	9.9	3.5	6.2	4.2	6.3	20.3	0.1	0.3	0.3	0.5	1.2
45-49	8.1	2.1	2.9	5.4	18.4	16.5	5.2	4.5	7.5	33.7	0.6	0.3	0.3	0.6	1.7
50-54	15.2	1.9	3.0	4.8	24.8	25.6	4.2	4.6	6.7	41.1	0.9	0.2	0.3	0.5	1.9
55-59	13.3	1.3	2.1	2.0	18.8	23.5	2.8	2.9	3.2	32.3	0.7	0.1	0.2	0.2	1.2
Total	37.9	8.0	15.3	34.5	95.6	69.2	20.6	21.7	42.9	154.3	2.3	1.0	1.3	2.5	7.1

CONTINUED

OUT OF SERVICE TEACHERS AGED UNDER 60

Qualified teachers out of service[1,2] at 31 March 1999 aged under 60 who were previously in service, by last known sector, calendar year of last service, sex and age at 31 March 1999[3]

ENGLAND ONLY

(thousands)

	Other[4]					Total				
	Calendar year of last service					Calendar year of last service				
	before 1983	1983 to 1987	1988 to 1992	1993 to 1999	all years	before 1983	1983 to 1987	1988 to 1992	1993 to 1999	all years
Men										
Under 25	-	-	-	-	-	-	-	-	0.2	0.2
Under 25	-	-	-	-	-	-	-	-	0.1	0.1
25-29	-	-	-	0.2	0.2	-	-	-	2.3	2.3
30-34	-	-	-	0.5	0.5	-	-	0.6	3.6	4.2
35-39	-	0.1	0.2	0.5	0.8	-	1.0	2.0	3.1	6.1
40-44	0.1	0.4	0.4	0.7	1.6	1.5	3.0	2.1	3.1	9.7
45-49	0.7	0.6	0.6	1.1	3.0	7.9	3.1	2.8	4.4	18.1
50-54	1.4	0.6	0.7	1.1	3.8	13.4	2.7	3.1	3.8	23.0
55-59	1.6	0.4	0.4	0.4	2.8	12.1	1.6	1.6	1.3	16.6
Total	3.9	2.1	2.3	4.5	12.7	34.9	11.4	12.0	21.9	80.2
Women										
Under 25	-	-	-	-	-	-	-	-	0.6	0.6
25-29	-	-	-	0.6	0.6	-	-	-	8.3	8.3
30-34	-	-	0.1	1.1	1.2	-	-	2.1	13.2	15.3
35-39	-	0.2	0.6	1.1	1.9	-	2.3	6.6	10.9	19.8
40-44	0.3	0.8	0.7	1.2	3.0	3.9	6.6	5.9	9.8	26.3
45-49	1.2	0.6	0.7	1.6	4.1	19.2	5.7	6.2	11.8	42.9
50-54	2.0	0.6	0.7	1.7	5.0	31.8	4.7	6.3	10.9	53.6
55-59	1.8	0.4	0.6	0.9	3.6	28.8	3.5	4.5	5.3	42.2
Total	5.3	2.6	3.3	8.1	19.4	83.7	22.9	31.8	70.6	208.9
Men and women										
Under 25	-	-	-	-	-	-	-	-	0.7	0.7
25-29	-	-	-	0.8	0.8	-	-	-	10.6	10.6
30-34	-	-	0.1	1.5	1.7	-	-	2.7	16.8	19.5
35-39	-	0.3	0.8	1.6	2.6	-	3.3	8.6	14.0	25.9
40-44	0.5	1.1	1.1	1.9	4.5	5.4	9.7	8.1	12.9	36.0
45-49	1.9	1.2	1.3	2.7	7.2	27.1	8.8	9.0	16.2	61.0
50-54	3.4	1.2	1.5	2.7	8.8	45.1	7.4	9.3	14.7	76.6
55-59	3.4	0.8	1.0	1.2	6.4	40.9	5.1	6.1	6.6	58.8
Total	9.2	4.6	5.6	12.6	32.1	118.5	34.3	43.8	92.5	289.1

Source: Database of Teacher Records.

1. Excluding those who are receiving a pension from the Teachers Pension Scheme (TPS).
2. Some in service teachers may be shown as not in service because their service details are not recorded. These may include qualified teachers in the 'old' university sector, teachers in the independent sector who are not members of the Teachers Pension Scheme (TPS), part-time teachers outside the maintained nursey, primary and secondary sector who are not members of the TPS.
3. Provisional data.
4. Other includes the independent sector, further and higher education.

OUT OF SERVICE TEACHERS AGED UNDER 60

Qualified teachers who have never been in service[1] up to 31 March 1999 aged under 60,
by calendar year qualified, sex and age at 31 March 1999[2]

ENGLAND AND WALES (thousands)

	Calendar year qualified									
	before 1983	1983 to 1987	1988 to 1992	1993	1994	1995	1996	1997	1998	all years
Men										
Under 25	.	.	.	.	.	.	.	0.1	0.4	0.4
25-29	.	.	.	0.2	0.3	0.6	0.7	0.8	0.8	3.3
30-34	.	0.1	1.2	0.3	0.3	0.3	0.3	0.3	0.3	3.2
35-39	0.1	1.4	1.1	0.1	0.2	0.2	0.2	0.2	0.2	3.7
40-44	3.6	0.7	0.5	0.1	0.1	0.1	0.1	0.1	0.1	5.4
45-49	5.5	0.3	0.3	0.1	0.1	0.1	0.1	0.1	0.1	6.5
50-54	3.4	0.1	0.2	.	0.1	0.1	0.1	.	.	4.1
55-59	1.5	.	0.1	.	.	.	.	.	.	1.7
Total	14.1	2.5	3.4	0.9	1.1	1.4	1.5	1.6	1.9	28.3
Women										
Under 25	.	.	.	.	.	.	.	0.3	1.2	1.5
25-29	.	.	0.1	0.4	0.9	1.3	1.7	1.8	1.7	7.8
30-34	.	0.1	2.6	0.6	0.5	0.6	0.5	0.5	0.5	6.0
35-39	0.5	2.6	1.5	0.2	0.2	0.3	0.3	0.3	0.4	6.4
40-44	10.3	0.9	0.7	0.1	0.2	0.3	0.3	0.3	0.3	13.3
45-49	9.5	0.3	0.5	0.1	0.1	0.2	0.2	0.2	0.1	11.2
50-54	4.4	0.2	0.4	0.1	0.1	0.1	0.1	0.1	0.1	5.4
55-59	2.2	0.1	0.2	.	.	.	.	.	.	2.5
Total	26.9	4.1	6.0	1.7	2.0	2.8	3.0	3.4	4.4	54.2
Men and women										
Under 25	.	.	.	.	.	.	.	0.4	1.6	1.9
25-29	.	.	0.1	0.6	1.2	1.8	2.4	2.5	2.5	11.1
30-34	.	0.2	3.8	0.9	0.9	0.9	0.9	0.8	0.9	9.2
35-39	0.6	4.0	2.6	0.4	0.4	0.5	0.5	0.5	0.6	10.1
40-44	13.9	1.5	1.2	0.2	0.3	0.4	0.4	0.4	0.5	18.7
45-49	15.0	0.5	0.8	0.2	0.2	0.3	0.2	0.2	0.2	17.7
50-54	7.9	0.3	0.6	0.1	0.1	0.1	0.1	0.1	0.1	9.5
55-59	3.7	0.2	0.3	.	.	.	.	.	.	4.3
Total	41.0	6.7	9.4	2.5	3.1	4.1	4.5	5.0	6.3	82.5

Source: Database of Teacher Records

1. Some in service teachers may be shown as not in service because their service details are not recorded. These may include
   qualified teachers in the 'old' university sector, teachers in the independent sector who are not members of the Teachers
   Pension Scheme (TPS), part-time teachers outside the maintained nursery, primary and secondary sector who are not
   members of the TPS.
2. Data are provisional.

OUT OF SERVICE TEACHERS AGED UNDER 60

Qualified teachers who have never been in service[1] up to 31 March 1999 aged under 60,
by calendar year qualified, sex and age at 31 March 1999[2]

ENGLAND ONLY   (thousands)

		Calendar year qualified								
	before 1983	1983 to 1987	1988 to 1992	1993	1994	1995	1996	1997	1998	all years
Men										
Under 25	-	-	-	-	-	-	-	0.1	0.3	0.4
25-29	-	-	-	0.1	0.3	0.5	0.6	0.7	0.7	3.0
30-34	-	-	1.0	0.3	0.3	0.3	0.3	0.3	0.3	2.9
35-39	0.1	1.3	0.9	0.1	0.1	0.2	0.2	0.2	0.2	3.3
40-44	3.6	0.6	0.4	0.1	0.1	0.1	0.1	0.1	0.1	5.3
45-49	5.5	0.2	0.2	0.1	0.1	0.1	0.1	0.1	0.1	6.4
50-54	3.4	0.1	0.2	-	0.1	0.1	0.1	-	-	4.0
55-59	1.5	-	0.1	-	-	-	-	-	-	1.7
Total	14.1	2.3	3.0	0.8	1.0	1.3	1.3	1.5	1.7	27.0
Women										
Under 25	-	-	-	-	-	-	-	0.3	1.1	1.3
25-29	-	-	0.1	0.4	0.8	1.1	1.5	1.6	1.5	6.8
30-34	-	0.1	2.3	0.5	0.5	0.5	0.5	0.4	0.5	5.4
35-39	0.5	2.4	1.3	0.2	0.2	0.3	0.3	0.3	0.3	5.8
40-44	10.3	0.8	0.6	0.1	0.2	0.2	0.2	0.3	0.3	13.1
45-49	9.5	0.3	0.5	0.1	0.1	0.2	0.1	0.2	0.1	11.1
50-54	4.4	0.2	0.4	0.1	0.1	0.1	0.1	0.1	0.1	5.3
55-59	2.2	0.1	0.1	-	-	-	-	-	-	2.5
Total	26.9	3.9	5.3	1.5	1.8	2.5	2.7	3.0	3.9	51.4
Men and women										
Under 25	-	-	-	-	-	-	-	0.3	1.4	1.7
25-29	-	-	0.1	0.5	1.0	1.6	2.1	2.2	2.2	9.8
30-34	-	0.2	3.4	0.8	0.8	0.9	0.8	0.7	0.8	8.3
35-39	0.6	3.7	2.2	0.4	0.3	0.5	0.4	0.5	0.5	9.2
40-44	13.9	1.4	1.0	0.2	0.3	0.4	0.3	0.4	0.4	18.3
45-49	15.0	0.5	0.7	0.2	0.2	0.3	0.2	0.2	0.2	17.5
50-54	7.9	0.2	0.6	0.1	0.1	0.1	0.1	0.1	0.1	9.3
55-59	3.7	0.1	0.2	-	-	-	-	-	-	4.2
Total	41.0	6.2	8.3	2.3	2.8	3.7	4.0	4.5	5.6	78.4

Source: Database of Teacher Records

1. Some in service teachers may be shown as not in service because their service details are not recorded. These may include
   qualified teachers in the 'old' university sector, teachers in the independent sector who are not members of the Teachers
   Pension Scheme (TPS), part-time teachers outside the maintained nursey, primary and secondary sector who are not
   members of the TPS.
2. Data are provisional.

52 FURTHER EDUCATION
Adult/community/youth centres[1]: 1995 to 2000 by type of centre and type of contract

ENGLAND ONLY

	1995	1996	1997	1998	1999	2000[2]
All lecturers	7,040	7,040	6,790	6,280	7,020	6,770
of which:						
Adult or community education centres	6,330	6,490	6,230	5,920	6,540	6,260
Youth clubs and centres	540	420	390	230	340	340
Elsewhere	170	140	160	130	140	170
Full-time	1,370	1,260	1,190	1,040	2,000	2,170
Part-time	5,670	5,780	5,600	5,240	5,010	4,600

Source: DfEE annual 618G survey.

1. Lecturers employed by local authorities to provide FE for adults or FE for young people as part of an authorities youth service.
2. Provisional data.

FURTHER EDUCATION

Further education: graduate status and degree subject of full-time lecturers by sex and age, 31 March 1999[1,2]

ENGLAND AND WALES

	Graduates[3]						Graduate status not known	All lecturers		
	Mathe-matics	Science (including medicine)	Tech-nology	Agri-culture	Other subjects	Total		Number	Percentage of total	Cumulative percentage
Men										
Under 25	-	-	-	-	20	20	20	40	0.2	0.2
25-29	50	50	10	10	300	420	320	740	2.7	2.8
30-34	90	160	50	20	710	1,030	940	1,960	7.1	10.0
35-39	130	270	80	30	1,080	1,580	1,570	3,150	11.5	21.5
40-44	170	460	170	30	1,670	2,510	2,300	4,810	17.5	39.0
45-49	310	720	280	50	2,590	3,950	2,970	6,920	25.2	64.3
50-54	250	650	320	40	2,170	3,430	3,060	6,490	23.7	87.9
55-59	70	280	100	20	690	1,160	1,370	2,520	9.2	97.1
60 and over	20	40	30	-	210	310	490	790	2.9	100
All ages	1,090	2,630	1,040	190	9,440	14,400	13,030	27,430	100	
Women										
Under 25	-	-	-	-	40	50	60	110	0.5	0.5
25-29	40	70	-	10	430	560	530	1,090	5.1	5.6
30-34	50	110	10	10	750	930	1,000	1,930	9.0	14.7
35-39	70	150	20	10	1,010	1,250	1,400	2,650	12.5	27.1
40-44	100	260	30	10	1,540	1,940	1,980	3,920	18.4	45.5
45-49	170	330	20	10	2,060	2,590	2,680	5,270	24.7	70.2
50-54	150	330	20	-	1,720	2,210	2,390	4,610	21.6	91.8
55-59	50	90	-	-	550	680	800	1,490	7.0	98.8
60 and over	10	10	-	-	90	110	150	250	1.2	100
All ages	640	1,350	100	60	8,170	10,320	11,000	21,320	100	
Men and Women										
Under 25	10	10	-	-	60	80	80	150	0.3	0.3
25-29	90	120	20	20	740	980	850	1,830	3.8	4.1
30-34	140	270	60	30	1,460	1,950	1,940	3,890	8.0	12.0
35-39	200	420	100	30	2,080	2,830	2,980	5,810	11.9	24.0
40-44	270	720	200	50	3,210	4,450	4,280	8,730	17.9	41.9
45-49	480	1,050	300	60	4,640	6,540	5,650	12,190	25.0	66.9
50-54	400	980	340	40	3,890	5,640	5,450	11,090	22.8	89.6
55-59	120	360	100	20	1,240	1,840	2,170	4,010	8.2	97.8
60 and over	30	50	30	-	300	410	640	1,050	2.2	100
All ages	1,730	3,990	1,140	260	17,610	24,720	24,020	48,740	100	

Source: Database of Teacher Records.

1. Provisional data.
2. Including sixth form colleges.
3. Including graduate equivalents.

53b

FURTHER EDUCATION

Further education: graduate status and degree subject of full-time lecturers by sex and age, 31 March 1999[1,2]

ENGLAND ONLY

	Graduates[3]						Graduate status not known	All lecturers		
	Mathematics	Science (including medicine)	Technology	Agriculture	Other subjects	Total		Number	Percentage of total	Cumulative percentage
Men										
Under 25	-	-	-	-	10	20	20	40	0.1	0.1
25-29	40	50	10	10	290	400	290	680	2.6	2.8
30-34	80	140	40	10	670	950	870	1,820	7.0	9.8
35-39	120	260	80	20	1,010	1,490	1,460	2,950	11.4	21.2
40-44	160	440	160	30	1,610	2,410	2,160	4,570	17.6	38.9
45-49	290	690	260	50	2,480	3,770	2,800	6,570	25.4	64.3
50-54	240	620	310	30	2,080	3,270	2,860	6,130	23.7	88.0
55-59	70	260	100	20	640	1,080	1,280	2,360	9.1	97.1
60 and over	20	40	30	-	210	290	460	750	2.9	100
All ages	1,030	2,500	990	180	9,000	13,690	12,190	25,880	100	
Women										
Under 25	-	-	-	-	40	50	50	100	0.5	0.5
25-29	40	70	-	10	400	520	500	1,020	5.1	5.6
30-34	50	100	10	10	700	870	930	1,800	8.9	14.5
35-39	70	140	20	10	950	1,180	1,320	2,500	12.4	27.0
40-44	100	250	30	10	1,450	1,830	1,860	3,690	18.4	45.4
45-49	160	320	20	10	1,950	2,450	2,530	4,980	24.8	70.2
50-54	140	310	20	-	1,620	2,080	2,260	4,340	21.6	91.8
55-59	50	80	-	-	520	650	760	1,410	7.0	98.8
60 and over	-	10	-	-	90	100	140	240	1.2	100
All ages	600	1,280	90	60	7,710	9,730	10,350	20,080	100	
Men and Women										
Under 25	10	10	-	-	50	70	70	140	0.3	0.3
25-29	80	120	20	20	690	920	790	1,700	3.7	4.0
30-34	130	240	50	30	1,370	1,820	1,800	3,620	7.9	11.9
35-39	180	400	90	30	1,970	2,670	2,780	5,450	11.9	23.7
40-44	260	690	190	40	3,060	4,240	4,020	8,260	18.0	41.7
45-49	450	1,010	280	60	4,430	6,220	5,330	11,550	25.1	66.8
50-54	380	920	320	40	3,690	5,360	5,120	10,470	22.8	89.6
55-59	120	350	100	20	1,160	1,740	2,040	3,780	8.2	97.8
60 and over	20	50	30	-	290	390	600	990	2.2	100
All ages	1,620	3,780	1,080	240	16,710	23,420	22,540	45,960	100	

Source: Database of Teacher Records.

1. Provisional data.
2. Including sixth form colleges.
3. Including graduate equivalents.

FURTHER EDUCATION
Full-time lecturers in further education, 31 March 1999: salary ranges by sex and age [1]

54a

ENGLAND AND WALES

	Up to £14,999	£15,000 -18,999	£19,000 -22,999	£23,000 -26,999	£27,000 -30,999	£31,000 -34,999	£35,000 and over	Salary not known	Total	Average Salary (£)
Men										
Under 25	10	20	-	-	-	-	-	-	40	15,860
25-29	60	420	170	50	-	-	-	50	740	18,300
30-34	40	500	790	400	70	10	-	130	1,960	20,930
35-39	30	370	890	1,140	370	60	40	250	3,160	23,440
40-44	50	290	940	2,030	790	200	170	340	4,810	25,090
45-49	30	210	1,090	2,930	1,340	360	520	450	6,920	26,650
50-54	20	170	900	2,620	1,410	360	580	430	6,490	27,360
55-59	10	60	330	1,020	550	130	280	160	2,520	27,930
60 and over	10	20	80	390	160	30	60	50	790	27,300
All ages	250	2,060	5,190	10,580	4,700	1,140	1,650	1,860	27,430	25,670
Women										
Under 25	50	50	-	-	-	-	-	10	110	15,490
25-29	80	640	250	50	-	-	-	70	1,090	18,140
30-34	50	520	720	400	70	10	-	160	1,930	20,850
35-39	50	380	840	820	280	50	40	200	2,650	22,910
40-44	50	390	1,070	1,410	520	110	110	270	3,920	24,000
45-49	50	350	1,210	2,120	790	210	200	340	5,270	24,940
50-54	30	200	860	1,940	840	190	240	300	4,610	25,770
55-59	10	60	270	650	270	80	70	80	1,490	25,930
60 and over	-	10	40	130	40	10	10	20	250	25,680
All ages	360	2,580	5,270	7,520	2,830	650	670	1,440	21,320	24,010
Men and Women										
Under 25	60	80	-	-	-	-	-	10	150	15,600
25-29	130	1,050	420	100	10	-	-	120	1,830	18,200
30-34	90	1,020	1,510	800	140	20	10	290	3,890	20,890
35-39	80	750	1,730	1,960	650	110	80	450	5,810	23,200
40-44	90	680	2,020	3,440	1,310	310	280	610	8,730	24,600
45-49	80	560	2,300	5,050	2,130	560	720	790	12,190	25,910
50-54	50	370	1,760	4,560	2,250	550	820	730	11,090	26,700
55-59	20	110	600	1,670	820	200	350	240	4,010	27,180
60 and over	10	30	120	520	210	40	70	60	1,050	26,910
All ages	620	4,640	10,460	18,100	7,520	1,790	2,320	3,300	48,750	24,940

Source: Database of Teacher Records.

1. Including sixth form colleges.

FURTHER EDUCATION

54b

Full-time lecturers in further education, 31 March 1999: salary ranges by sex and age [1]

ENGLAND ONLY

	Up to £14,999	£15,000 -18,999	£19,000 -22,999	£23,000 -26,999	£27,000 -30,999	£31,000 -34,999	£35,000 and over	Salary not known	Total	Average Salary (£)
Men										
Under 25	10	20	-	-	-	-	-	-	40	15,960
25-29	50	370	170	50	-	-	-	40	680	18,390
30-34	40	460	720	390	70	10	-	130	1,820	21,030
35-39	30	340	820	1,060	360	60	40	240	2,950	23,480
40-44	40	270	900	1,890	770	180	160	340	4,570	25,140
45-49	30	200	1,050	2,740	1,290	340	490	440	6,570	26,680
50-54	10	160	860	2,420	1,350	340	570	420	6,130	27,430
55-59	10	50	310	930	520	120	260	160	2,360	28,000
60 and over	10	20	80	350	160	30	60	50	750	27,420
All ages	230	1,900	4,910	9,830	4,530	1,070	1,590	1,830	25,880	25,740
Women										
Under 25	40	50	-	-	-	-	-	10	100	15,520
25-29	70	590	240	50	-	-	-	70	1,020	18,200
30-34	50	470	680	370	70	10	-	150	1,800	20,900
35-39	40	350	790	770	270	50	40	190	2,500	22,940
40-44	50	360	1,010	1,320	510	100	100	260	3,690	24,070
45-49	50	320	1,150	1,970	770	190	200	340	4,980	25,010
50-54	30	180	820	1,800	810	190	230	300	4,340	25,820
55-59	10	50	250	610	260	70	70	80	1,410	25,970
60 and over	-	10	40	120	40	10	10	20	240	25,740
All ages	340	2,380	4,960	6,990	2,730	610	650	1,420	20,080	24,080
Men and Women										
Under 25	50	70	-	-	-	-	-	10	140	15,640
25-29	120	970	400	100	10	-	-	110	1,700	18,280
30-34	80	920	1,400	760	140	20	10	280	3,620	20,970
35-39	80	690	1,610	1,830	630	100	80	440	5,450	23,230
40-44	90	630	1,900	3,210	1,280	280	270	610	8,260	24,660
45-49	80	510	2,190	4,710	2,060	530	690	780	11,550	25,960
50-54	40	350	1,680	4,210	2,150	520	790	720	10,470	26,760
55-59	20	110	570	1,540	780	190	330	240	3,780	27,240
60 and over	10	30	120	470	200	40	70	60	990	27,010
All ages	570	4,270	9,870	16,830	7,260	1,690	2,230	3,240	45,970	25,010

Source: Database of Teacher Records.

1. Including sixth form colleges.

FURTHER EDUCATION

55

Retirements from further education establishments: type of award by year of retirement, new[1] and current[2] awards and average benefits[3] awarded

ENGLAND AND WALES

	Premature			Age		
	Men	Women	All	Men	Women	All
1995-96						
New[1] awards						
Number	1,990	740	2,730	410	180	590
Average benefits[3]	£8,400	£5,800	£7,700	£7,400	£4,500	£6,500
Current[2] awards	20,740	6,140	26,880	8,580	3,130	11,710
1996-97						
New[1] awards						
Number	2,560	1,090	3,660	370	160	530
Average benefits[3]	£8,500	£6,200	£7,800	£6,600	£3,900	£5,800
Current[2] awards	23,040	7,180	30,230	8,560	3,150	11,710
1997-98						
New[1] awards						
Number	2,270	1,280	3,540	360	210	570
Average benefits[3]	£8,700	£6,000	£7,800	£7,700	£3,700	£6,200
Current[2] awards	25,090	8,470	33,560	9,000	4,470	13,470
1998-99 [4]						
New[1] awards						
Number	50	20	80	410	240	650
Average benefits3	£8,800	£7,000	£8,200	£6,900	£4,400	£6,000
Current[2] awards	24,790	8,430	33,220	9,020	4,590	13,610
1999-00 [4]						
New[1] awards						
Number	60	30	90	420	270	680
Average benefits[3]	£9,900	£5,100	£8,300	£7,600	£4,100	£6,300
Current[2] awards	24,460	8,380	32,840	8,730	4,480	13,210
1999-00 England only [4]						
New[1] awards						
Number	50	30	80	400	260	660
Average benefits[3]	£10,100	£5,000	£8,400	£7,600	£4,200	£6,300
Current[2] awards	22,940	7,890	30,830	8,390	4,330	12,720

CONTINUED
FURTHER EDUCATION
Retirements from further education establishments: type of award by year of retirement, new[1] and current[2] awards and average benefits[3] awarded
ENGLAND AND WALES

	Ill-health			Total		
	Men	Women	All	Men	Women	All
1995-96						
New[1] awards						
Number	440	250	690	2,840	1,170	4,010
Average benefits[3]	£8,200	£6,700	£7,700	£8,200	£5,800	£7,500
Current[2] awards	3,220	1,690	4,910	32,540	10,960	43,500
1996-97						
New[1] awards						
Number	410	300	710	3,350	1,550	4,900
Average benefits[3]	£8,100	£6,800	£7,500	£8,300	£6,100	£7,600
Current[2] awards	3,570	1,970	5,540	35,170	12,300	47,470
1997-98						
New[1] awards						
Number	310	250	560	2,930	1,740	4,670
Average benefits[3]	£8,200	£6,800	£7,600	£8,600	£5,900	£7,600
Current[2] awards	3,930	2,280	6,200	38,020	15,210	53,230
1998-99 [4]						
New[1] awards						
Number	190	120	310	660	380	1,030
Average benefits[3]	£8,100	£6,100	£7,300	£7,400	£5,000	£6,500
Current[2] awards	4,060	2,380	6,440	37,880	15,400	53,280
1999-00 [4]						
New[1] awards						
Number	170	120	300	650	420	1,070
Average benefits[3]	£8,900	£6,600	£8,000	£8,200	£4,900	£6,900
Current[2] awards	4,040	2,400	6,440	37,240	15,260	52,490
1999-00 England only [4]						
New[1] awards						
Number	160	120	280	620	400	1,020
Average benefits[3]	£9,000	£6,600	£8,000	£8,200	£5,000	£6,900
Current[2] awards	3,820	2,250	6,070	35,150	14,470	49,620

Source: Database of Teacher Records and Pensioner Statistical System (PENSTATS).

1. 'New' is defined as those awarded retirement benefits in the financial year shown.
2. 'Current' includes teachers awarded retirement benefits in the current financial year plus those awarded benefits in a previous financial year and who are still receiving benefits up to the end of the years shown.
3. This is the average of the annual pension and does not include the one-off 'lump-sum' payments.
4. Provisional data.

HIGHER EDUCATION

Full-time lecturers in higher education: graduate status and degree subject by sex and age, 31 March 1999 [1,2]

56a

ENGLAND AND WALES

	Graduates [3]						Graduate status not known	All teachers		
	Mathe-matics	Science (Including medicine)	Tech-nology	Agri-culture	Other subjects	Total		Number	Percentage of total	Cumulative percentage
Men										
Under 25	-	-	-	-	-	10	10	20	0.1	0.1
25-29	20	30	10	-	130	190	170	360	2.2	2.3
30-34	50	120	50	10	380	610	630	1,230	7.5	9.7
35-39	70	190	100	10	600	960	930	1,890	11.5	21.2
40-44	100	240	150	-	840	1,330	1,140	2,470	15.0	36.3
45-49	180	320	220	10	1,390	2,110	1,360	3,480	21.1	57.4
50-54	240	430	290	10	1,610	2,580	1,550	4,120	25.0	82.4
55-59	120	300	160	10	740	1,320	850	2,170	13.1	95.6
60 and over	30	110	50	-	250	440	290	730	4.4	100
All ages	810	1,740	1,020	60	5,930	9,550	6,910	16,470	100	
Women										
Under 25	-	-	-	-	-	-	10	10	0.1	0.1
25-29	10	20	-	-	110	150	170	320	3.7	3.8
30-34	20	70	10	10	370	480	480	950	10.9	14.7
35-39	30	100	20	-	470	620	710	1,330	15.3	30.0
40-44	30	120	10	-	660	820	870	1,690	19.4	49.4
45-49	60	120	20	10	830	1,020	940	1,970	22.6	72.0
50-54	50	120	10	-	670	860	800	1,650	19.0	91.0
55-59	10	40	-	-	270	320	300	620	7.1	98.2
60 and over	-	10	-	-	70	80	80	160	1.8	100
All ages	220	590	70	20	3,460	4,350	4,350	8,710	100	
Men and Women										
Under 25	-	-	-	-	10	10	20	30	0.1	0.1
25-29	30	50	10	-	240	340	340	680	2.7	2.8
30-34	70	190	50	10	760	1,080	1,100	2,190	8.7	11.5
35-39	100	290	120	20	1,060	1,580	1,640	3,220	12.8	24.3
40-44	140	360	160	-	1,490	2,150	2,010	4,170	16.5	40.8
45-49	230	440	230	10	2,220	3,140	2,310	5,440	21.6	62.4
50-54	290	550	300	20	2,290	3,440	2,340	5,780	22.9	85.4
55-59	130	330	170	10	1,010	1,640	1,140	2,790	11.1	96.5
60 and over	30	120	50	-	320	520	370	890	3.5	100
All ages	1,020	2,330	1,090	80	9,390	13,900	11,270	25,170	100	

Source: Database of Teacher Records.

1. Provisional data.
2. Not all higher education lecturers are shown because they are not all members of the Teachers Pension Scheme. The total number of full-time lecturers employed by institutions in the higher education sector in England and Wales in 1998/99, as recorded by the Higher Education Statistics Agency's Individualised Staff Record, was 95,600.
3. Including graduate equivalents.

56b

ENGLAND ONLY

	Graduates [3]						Graduate status not known	All teachers		
	Mathe-matics	Science (Including medicine)	Tech-nology	Agri-culture	Other subjects	Total		Number	Percentage of total	Cumulative percentage
Men										
Under 25	-	-	-	-	-	10	10	10	0.1	0.1
25-29	20	30	10	-	130	180	160	340	2.2	2.3
30-34	50	120	50	10	360	580	580	1,160	7.5	9.8
35-39	60	180	90	10	550	890	870	1,760	11.4	21.2
40-44	100	230	130	-	780	1,230	1,070	2,310	14.9	36.2
45-49	170	300	190	10	1,290	1,960	1,290	3,250	21.1	57.2
50-54	220	400	260	10	1,510	2,410	1,450	3,860	25.0	82.2
55-59	110	280	150	10	700	1,240	800	2,040	13.2	95.5
60 and over	30	110	40	-	240	420	280	700	4.5	100
All ages	750	1,640	920	50	5,560	8,910	6,520	15,430	100	
Women										
Under 25	-	-	-	-	-	-	10	10	0.1	0.1
25-29	10	20	-	-	100	140	160	300	3.7	3.8
30-34	20	70	10	10	350	450	450	900	10.9	14.7
35-39	30	100	20	-	440	580	680	1,260	15.3	30.0
40-44	30	120	10	-	610	760	830	1,590	19.4	49.4
45-49	50	110	20	10	780	960	890	1,850	22.6	72.0
50-54	50	110	10	-	640	810	760	1,570	19.1	91.1
55-59	10	30	-	-	250	300	280	580	7.0	98.1
60 and over	-	10	-	-	70	80	70	150	1.9	100
All ages	200	570	60	20	3,230	4,080	4,130	8,220	100	
Men and Women										
Under 25	-	-	-	-	10	10	10	20	0.1	0.1
25-29	30	50	10	-	230	320	320	640	2.7	2.8
30-34	70	180	50	10	710	1,020	1,030	2,050	8.7	11.5
35-39	90	280	110	20	990	1,480	1,550	3,020	12.8	24.3
40-44	130	350	130	-	1,380	1,990	1,910	3,900	16.5	40.8
45-49	220	410	210	10	2,070	2,920	2,180	5,100	21.6	62.4
50-54	270	510	270	10	2,150	3,220	2,220	5,430	23.0	85.3
55-59	120	310	150	10	950	1,540	1,080	2,620	11.1	96.4
60 and over	30	120	40	-	310	500	350	850	3.6	100
All ages	950	2,200	980	70	8,790	12,990	10,650	23,640	100	

Source: Database of Teacher Records.

1. Provisional data.
2. Not all higher education lecturers are shown because they are not all members of the Teachers Pension Scheme. The total number of full-time lecturers employed by institutions in the higher education sector in England in 1998/99, as recorded by the Higher Education Statistics Agency's Individualised Staff Record, was 90,200.
3. Including graduate equivalents.

HIGHER EDUCATION
Full-time lecturers in higher education: salary ranges by sex and age, 31 March 1999 [1,2]

57a

ENGLAND AND WALES

	Up to £14,999	£15,000 -18,999	£19,000 -22,999	£23,000 -26,999	£27,000 -30,999	£31,000 -34,999	£35,000 and over	Salary not known	Total	Average Salary (£)
Men										
Under 25	-	10	-	-	-	-	-	-	20	16,840
25-29	10	130	140	60	-	-	-	10	360	19,870
30-34	10	90	400	440	180	30	10	70	1,230	23,820
35-39	-	20	230	530	710	190	120	90	1,890	27,710
40-44	-	30	90	340	1,160	420	310	130	2,470	30,110
45-49	-	10	70	200	1,540	600	910	150	3,480	32,440
50-54	-	-	30	130	1,620	670	1,510	170	4,120	34,040
55-59	-	-	20	40	860	310	850	90	2,170	34,580
60 and over	-	-	-	20	280	120	280	30	730	33,770
All ages	30	290	980	1,750	6,350	2,350	3,980	730	16,470	31,370
Women										
Under 25	-	10	-	-	-	-	-	-	10	15,960
25-29	20	110	130	40	-	-	-	10	320	19,660
30-34	10	70	300	330	170	10	-	60	950	23,700
35-39	-	30	160	410	530	100	40	60	1,330	26,930
40-44	-	20	100	260	860	250	130	80	1,690	29,140
45-49	-	30	70	260	880	350	270	110	1,970	30,280
50-54	-	10	30	140	750	300	340	90	1,650	31,760
55-59	-	-	10	30	260	130	170	30	620	32,820
60 and over	-	-	-	10	60	40	50	-	160	32,730
All ages	40	280	800	1,480	3,510	1,170	980	450	8,710	28,930
Men and Women										
Under 25	10	20	-	-	-	-	-	-	30	16,500
25-29	30	240	270	100	10	-	-	30	680	19,770
30-34	20	160	710	770	350	40	20	130	2,190	23,770
35-39	10	50	390	940	1,240	300	150	150	3,220	27,390
40-44	-	50	190	600	2,020	670	430	220	4,170	29,710
45-49	-	40	130	470	2,420	950	1,180	250	5,440	31,670
50-54	-	10	60	270	2,370	970	1,840	260	5,780	33,390
55-59	-	-	30	60	1,110	440	1,020	120	2,790	34,180
60 and over	-	-	10	30	340	160	320	30	890	33,590
All ages	70	560	1,780	3,230	9,860	3,530	4,970	1,180	25,170	30,530

Source: Database of Teacher Records.

1. Provisional data.
2. Not all higher education lecturers are shown because they are not all members of the Teachers Pension Scheme. The total number of full-time lecturers employed by institutions in the higher education sector in England and Wales in 1998/99, as recorded by the Higher Education Statistics Agency's Individualised Staff Record, was 95,600.

HIGHER EDUCATION

Full-time lecturers in higher education: salary ranges by sex and age, 31 March 1999 [1,2]

ENGLAND ONLY

	Up to £14,999	£15,000 -18,999	£19,000 -22,999	£23,000 -26,999	£27,000 -30,999	£31,000 -34,999	£35,000 and over	Salary not known	Total	Average Salary (£)
Men										
Under 25	-	10	-	-	-	-	-	-	10	16,390
25-29	10	120	130	60	-	-	-	10	340	19,890
30-34	10	80	380	410	170	30	10	70	1,160	23,860
35-39	-	20	220	490	660	190	110	90	1,760	27,750
40-44	-	20	80	320	1,060	400	280	130	2,310	30,170
45-49	-	10	60	180	1,400	590	870	140	3,250	32,550
50-54	-	-	30	110	1,480	650	1,430	160	3,860	34,160
55-59	-	-	20	30	790	310	800	90	2,040	34,650
60 and over	-	-	-	20	270	120	260	30	700	33,650
All ages	30	260	920	1,610	5,840	2,290	3,760	720	15,430	31,450
Women										
Under 25	-	10	-	-	-	-	-	-	10	15,950
25-29	10	110	120	40	-	-	-	10	300	19,770
30-34	10	70	280	310	160	10	-	60	900	23,770
35-39	-	30	150	390	490	100	30	60	1,260	26,950
40-44	-	10	90	240	800	250	120	80	1,590	29,210
45-49	-	20	60	230	840	340	260	110	1,850	30,430
50-54	-	10	20	130	710	290	320	90	1,570	31,840
55-59	-	-	10	20	230	120	160	30	580	33,080
60 and over	-	-	-	10	60	30	40	-	150	32,720
All ages	30	260	730	1,370	3,290	1,150	940	450	8,220	29,020
Men and Women										
Under 25	10	10	-	-	-	-	-	-	20	16,220
25-29	30	230	250	100	10	-	-	30	640	19,830
30-34	20	140	660	720	330	40	10	130	2,050	23,820
35-39	10	50	360	880	1,150	290	140	150	3,020	27,410
40-44	-	40	170	560	1,860	650	400	220	3,900	29,780
45-49	-	30	120	410	2,240	930	1,120	250	5,100	31,790
50-54	-	10	50	230	2,190	940	1,750	260	5,430	33,500
55-59	-	-	20	50	1,020	430	970	120	2,620	34,310
60 and over	-	-	-	30	330	150	310	30	850	33,480
All ages	60	520	1,650	2,980	9,130	3,430	4,700	1,170	23,640	30,610

Source: Database of Teacher Records.

1. Provisional data.
2. Not all higher education lecturers are shown because they are not all members of the Teachers Pension Scheme. The total number of full-time lecturers employed by institutions in the higher education sector in England in 1998/99, as recorded by the Higher Education Statistics Agency's Individualised Staff Record, was 90,200.

HIGHER EDUCATION

Retirements from higher education establishments [1]: type of award by year of retirement, new [2] and current [3] awards and average benefits [4] awarded

ENGLAND AND WALES

	Premature			Age		
	Men	Women	All	Men	Women	All
1995-96						
New [2] awards						
Number	460	120	580	190	40	230
Average benefits [4]	£10,400	£8,800	£10,100	£9,500	£6,900	£9,000
Current [3] awards	7,300	1,450	8,750	2,160	500	2,660
1996-97						
New [2] awards						
Number	770	180	950	220	60	280
Average benefits [4]	£11,300	£9,200	£10,900	£9,700	£6,500	£9,000
Current [3] awards	8,030	1,620	9,650	2,320	560	2,870
1997-98						
New [2] awards						
Number	1,160	410	1,560	270	60	330
Average benefits [4]	£11,000	£9,000	£10,500	£10,800	£7,100	£10,100
Current [3] awards	8,070	1,830	9,900	2,530	670	3,200
1998-99 [5]						
New [2] awards						
Number	100	20	120	250	90	340
Average benefits [4]	£11,200	£10,000	£10,900	£11,200	£7,700	£10,300
Current [3] awards	6,690	1,630	8,310	2,250	660	2,910
1999-00 [5]						
New [2] awards						
Number	80	30	100	260	80	330
Average benefits [4]	£12,100	£9,000	£11,300	£10,900	£7,900	£10,200
Current [3] awards	6,610	1,610	8,220	2,150	650	2,790
1999-00 England only [5]						
New [2] awards						
Number	70	20	90	250	80	320
Average benefits [4]	£12,700	£8,600	£11,700	£10,800	£7,800	£10,100
Current [3] awards	6,470	1,590	8,060	2,110	640	2,740

CONTINUED
HIGHER EDUCATION
Retirements from higher education establishments [1]: type of award by year of retirement, new [2] and current [3] awards and average benefits [4] awarded
ENGLAND AND WALES

	Ill-health			Total		
	Men	Women	All	Men	Women	All
1995-96						
New [2] awards						
Number	80	50	130	730	210	940
Average benefits [4]	£10,000	£8,700	£9,500	£10,100	£8,300	£9,700
Current [3] awards	590	240	830	10,040	2,190	12,230
1996-97						
New [2] awards						
Number	80	60	140	1,080	300	1,370
Average benefits [4]	£10,600	£9,400	£10,100	£10,900	£8,700	£10,400
Current [3] awards	650	300	960	11,000	2,480	13,480
1997-98						
New [2] awards						
Number	90	60	140	1,510	520	2,030
Average benefits [4]	£11,500	£9,200	£10,600	£11,000	£8,800	£10,400
Current [3] awards	720	330	1,050	11,310	2,840	14,150
1998-99 [5]						
New [2] awards						
Number	50	40	80	400	150	540
Average benefits [4]	£10,300	£8,100	£9,300	£11,100	£8,200	£10,300
Current [3] awards	620	310	930	9,550	2,600	12,150
1999-00 [5]						
New [2] awards						
Number	60	30	90	390	140	530
Average benefits [4]	£11,300	£9,100	£10,500	£11,200	£8,400	£10,500
Current [3] awards	620	310	930	9,370	2,570	11,950
1999-00 England only [5]						
New [2] awards						
Number	50	30	90	370	130	500
Average benefits [4]	£11,300	£9,200	£10,500	£11,200	£8,300	£10,500
Current [3] awards	600	300	900	9,170	2,520	11,700

Source: Database of Teacher Records and Pensioner Statistical System (PENSTATS).

1. Only retirements from the Teachers Pension Scheme are recorded in this table.
2. 'New' is defined as those awarded retirement benefits in the financial year shown.
3. 'Current' includes teachers awarded retirement benefits in the current financial year plus those awarded benefits in a previous financial year and who are still receiving benefits up to the end of the years shown.
4. This is the average of the annual pension and does not include the one-off 'lump-sum' payments.
5. Provisional data.